# CHINA
# modern

## Ching-He Huang

# CHINA
# modern

100 cutting-edge, fusion-style recipes for the 21st century

**Ching-He Huang**

**Photography by Kate Whitaker**

**Kyle Cathie Ltd**

**To my grandmother, mother, and all who have helped me on my culinary path.**

First published in Great Britain in 2006 by
Kyle Cathie Limited
23 Howland Street, London W1T 4AY
general.enquiries@kyle-cathie.com
www.kylecathie.com

10 9 8 7 6 5 4

ISBN 978 1 85626 961 2

*Project editor*: Stephanie Evans
*Designer*: Lucy Gowans
*Photographer*: Kate Whitaker, except for pp2, 5, 28, 39, 63, 67 © Gus Filgate
*Food stylist*: Annie Nichols
*Props stylist*: Wei Tang
*Production*: Sha Huxtable and Alice Holloway

A Cataloguing In Publication record for this title is available from the British Library.

Colour reproduction by Sang Choy
Printed and bound in Singapore by Star Standard

**Kyle Cathie Ltd**
23 Howland Street
London W1T 4AY
Tel: 020 7692 7215
general.enquiries@kyle-cathie.com
www.kylecathie.com

# Contents

# Introduction

Everyone knows that China is modernising and becoming open to Western ideas. Young Chinese are exposed to the wider world in ways their parents and certainly their grandparents could never imagine, with many working, living or travelling outside their vast homeland. This exchange of ideas is having a real impact on not only China's economy but on our very lifeforce: what we eat. It's a healthy sign. And China has a tremendous appetite for good tastes. Just as Chinese restaurants proliferated in Europe and America during the twentieth century, we now have fusion-style restaurants opening in Shanghai and Beijing. Chinese cuisine is set for an exciting journey.

I want to explore modern Chinese cooking in the hope of challenging conventional Western perceptions of Chinese food. I'll be reinventing the classics, challenging the view that Chinese food is no more than what any local takeaway is serving, and looking to the rest of Asia for inspiration to see how other great cuisines have influenced real Chinese food – and vice versa. This is a rather different cookbook from the 'norm'.

## Out of the wok, into the fire

In Britain, where I live now, cooking Chinese food at home is not as popular as, say, Italian cookery. Take a look at the supermarket ingredients aisles of these two sections, and you'll see what I mean. Is this because people view Chinese cookery as complicated and the ingredients inaccessible? This is a myth I want to dispel and I hope this book will demonstrate how easy it is to create healthy, sexy and delicious Chinese dishes. I've got recipes for everyone, any day of the week, whether you are feeling tired and lazy or up for a challenge!

First, I show you my take on the Chinese takeaway. The dishes will sound familiar but I've updated them in line with how I like to eat, adding a new twist to old favourites. In the second section, I'm going to broaden your experience to show you some of the real food of China. To me, traditional Chinese food means good home cooking using dishes that have been passed down the generations, so I'm going to share with you some of my family recipes. There's a world of Chinese home cooking unknown to the West… until now.

Then, the really fun part, bridging the gap between East and West. Nothing can be too quirky and I adore being adventurous. For all fun-loving cooks out there, this pushes the concept of modern Chinese to the limit. And the fusion is not just East and West. The last section focuses on East meeting East. For centuries, all the countries of Asia have influenced one another's cooking in terms of flavours and ingredients: fusion has to be an Asian concept! Truly sexy and exotic is how I describe these dishes.

I love the fact that Chinese cuisine is so versatile and there are so many different facets to it. I hope to inspire others to keep experimenting too and to think outside the box. There's nothing more exciting than discovering and reinventing, it keeps the soul alive, and the taste buds tantalised. This is modernisation: creating a new and delicious combination or adding your own flavour – make it yours.

# Happy cooking! *Ching 僧 Huang x*

# The Lowdown on Woks and Chinese Cooking Techniques

For centuries the Chinese have cooked with woks. It all started with conserving fuel. Stir frying is a clever way of cooking fast and hot, using the minimum of oil and retaining maximum nutrients in the food. The traditional cast iron woks are quite heavy and require seasoning. Those made from lighter carbon steel and non-stick electric woks are quite good. Some are two-handled to keep the wok stable, or you can buy a wok rest for use on gas hobs; this too helps keep the wok steady. The long wooden handle on a traditional wok allows you to hold the wok lightly in one hand while you hold a metal charn or wooden spoon in the other. This way you can manoeuvre the food quickly so that it doesn't burn.

To season a traditional cast iron wok, you need to clean it thoroughly first, because it is coated in oil prior to use. Place it on the hob to heat, add a little oil then rub kitchen paper over the entire surface (hold the paper with tongs – it will get hot!) to create a blackened effect. After use, scrub the wok with a damp towel or wooden brush, not a metal scourer or iron wool or you will remove the seasoning (unless of course you have burnt your food, then you will need to re-season it…). If you have never tried using a traditional wok, I would really recommend it because there is a real pleasure from making an authentic stir fry releasing the *wok-hei* or 'smoky wok flavour'.

**Stir frying** is the ultimate classic wok experience. A touch of oil and rapid stirring ensures that the ingredients retain their crunch and take on a smoky flavour. Yum. I'll share with you several tips to ensure success. Prepare all the ingredients in advance because once you start cooking, you won't have time! Cut meat and vegetables into even-sized pieces – that way, they cook in the same time and retain their juices. Cut leafy vegetables on the diagonal; exposing more surface to the heat means they cook faster. Prepare the wok by heating it first, then add the oil and swirl it around until it starts to smoke. Throw in the Chinese essentials (garlic and ginger) first, followed by meat or seafood and then the vegetables. This order of cooking helps to retain the bite of the vegetables. Keep the ingredients dry so that the oil does not spit, and because you're making a stir fry, not a stew. Or, if you want a saucy stir fry and use marinated meat, reserve the marinade until the very end of the process to be sure it doesn't all evaporate. Cooked noodles too are added at the end, along with the seasoning. Throughout the cooking, keep an eye on the level of heat in the wok. It should be high enough to sear the food but not burn it. You may need to adjust the flame because the temperature falls in the wok when ingredients are added. Another trick is to stir fry the meat first then set it to one side, cook all the vegetables then return the meat to the dish before adding the seasoning! I learned this one from my grandmother, a rather perfectionist cook!

**Steaming** is another great use for your wok. You can fill it half full with water and put the base of a bamboo steamer inside, with your food directly in the basket or on a plate that sits inside it. Put the lid on and steam to your heart's content! Steaming is a wonderfully healthy way of preparing a meal, and it's fast and fun, too. The basket gives a subtle bamboo fragrance to your food, it helps to keep the food warm once cooked, and is a stylish way of presenting your food at the table. Bamboo steamers vary in size, so make sure that you buy one that sits snug across the wok because you don't want the water to touch the base of the steamer. To cook a feast, you can pile the steamers up (though you need a powerful flame to induce enough steam to reach the highest basket, I say two or three piled high should be OK). My final tip is: turn off the gas before you remove the lid. I have been unwary or impatient too many times and burnt my hands and arms in the hot steam.

**Deep frying** is not considered a healthy cooking technique, but if the oil is hot enough, when the food is dropped into it the outer edges are quickly sealed, minimising the amount of oil that seeps into the food but you still get all the crispness and flavour. A handy purchase is a fab utensil called a spider, a steel mesh scoop which is sold in different sizes in all good Chinese supermarkets. Use the spider to lift and drain food and transfer it to plates lined with kitchen paper to soak up the excess oil. For best results, I'd recommend a deep-frying thermometer to get the oil temperature right, but you can apply the bread test I refer to in the recipes. My other golden rules are: ensure the wok is stable (use a wok stand or a flat-bottomed wok with two handles); don't tip in too much oil (less than half full) to lessen the chances of it bubbling and spilling; make sure the food is dry to prevent it from spitting; and never re-use oil. To keep the food hot, place it in a preheated oven before serving. Finally, use a cooking oil with a high heating point such as groundnut or corn oil – keep your sesame oil for seasoning. **Enjoy!**

# 1. Modern Takeaway Favourites

Chinese cuisine is the second most popular cuisine in the UK and you may wonder how this has come to be. It all started with the local Chinese takeaway of course. You can find one on almost any high street; the only difference being good or bad. The owners of some are out to make a quick buck whereas others really pride themselves on the dishes they create. I praise those in the latter category, because I despair whenever I have a bad takeaway experience.

Food-lovers all over the world are becoming increasingly aware that what they put into their mouths affects their health and well-being and, laden with bad press, Chinese takeaways and restaurants will have to take action. A revolution has to take place to wipe off MSG and artificial sauces from the menus – but this will be a major task. Far better, I believe, to follow what my grandmother advised: 'The best way to watch what you eat is to cook and prepare the food yourself.' She was not only a fabulous cook but extremely wise too, and she is the influence behind this chapter.

Here I have created dishes that we all know and love but I've given each one a few modern twists. I have also tried to limit the use of prepared sauces in these recipes to demonstrate that it is possible to create tasty, healthy Chinese dishes. I like to think that dishes such as my Steamed Pork and Prawn Siu Mai Dumplings, or Beef and Chilli Bamboo Shoots in Little Gem Lettuce, along with Nutty Chicken Cool Noodle Salad and Bacon and Egg-fried Rice are a true testament to the cause. In addition, I have made sure they are easy to prepare so that you can create your own Chinese takeaway experience at home under your own health-conscious eyes. (For those who are not so watchful, the Kung Po Chicken and Peking Duck are a must!)

# Sweet and Sour Chicken Sticks   serves 4/makes 8–10 skewers

400g skinless chicken breast, thinly sliced
400g tinned pineapple chunks, drained
1 red pepper, cut into chunks
1 green pepper, cut into chunks
1 onion, cut into wedges

for the marinade
1 tablespoon ground cinnamon
1 tablespoon ground cumin
1 teaspoon ground black pepper
150ml olive oil
100ml light soy sauce
2 tablespoons brown sugar

for the sweet and sour sauce
1 teaspoon sesame oil
1 garlic clove, crushed and finely chopped
1 tablespoon freshly grated ginger
2 tablespoons light soy sauce
1 tablespoon white wine vinegar
2 teaspoons rice vinegar
2 tablespoons ketchup
20ml pineapple juice
2 tablespoons brown sugar
2 tablespoons clear honey
1 tablespoon cornflour blended with
    2 tablespoons water
1 tablespoon chilli sauce (optional)
pinch of sea salt and ground white pepper

8–10 bamboo skewers, soaked in water to prevent
    them burning

I love sweet and sour chicken but it is always done as a stir fry. So, challenging the norm, I decided to make sweet and sour chicken skewers. Here, slices of chicken are marinated with spices then skewered with alternating chunks of pineapple, peppers and onions. Whether the chicken is then baked, grilled or barbecued on a summer's day, you must dip it into this delicious homemade sweet and sour sauce. The recipe may look lengthy, but it's not difficult, and you can always compromise and go for ready-made sweet and sour dipping sauce if you don't have time to make your own.

Preparation time: **15 minutes plus marinating**
Cooking time: **30 minutes**

1. Combine all the marinade ingredients in a bowl and add the chicken. Leave to marinate for as long as possible, overnight is best.
2. Preheat the oven to 180°C/350°F/Gas Mark 4 or preheat the grill to medium-high.
3. Thread the skewers with chicken slices and chunks of pineapple, peppers and onions. Place on a baking tray and cook for 20 minutes. If grilling, allow about 10 minutes, turning frequently.
4. Meanwhile, make the sweet and sour sauce. Heat a wok over high heat and add the sesame oil. Stir fry the garlic and ginger for less than 1 minute and then add in the rest of the ingredients down to the honey. Once the sauce starts to boil, add the blended cornflour and bring back to the boil, stirring well, until it thickens. Add a splash of chilli sauce if you wish and season with salt and pepper to taste. Place in a heatproof bowl, cover and keep warm in the oven.
5. When the chicken is cooked, serve immediately with the sweet and sour sauce for dipping.

# Peking Duck and Rice Paper Rolls   makes about 24

*1 whole medium duck*
*2 litres boiling water*

*for the glaze*
*5 tablespoons clear honey*
*2 tablespoons dark soy sauce*
*4 tablespoons five-spice powder*
*2 tablespoons brown sugar*

*for the Peking duck sauce*
*2 tablespoons sesame oil*
*6 tablespoons hoi sin sauce*
*6 tablespoons caster sugar*
*6 tablespoons water*
*1 tablespoon dark soy sauce*
*1 tablespoon cornflour blended with*
*    1 tablespoon cold water*

*24 rice paper rolls*
*3 spring onions, sliced into long thin strips*
*1 cucumber, deseeded and sliced into*
*    long thin strips*

This is one of my all-time favourite recipes, one enjoyed by my family and friends on numerous occasions! You can buy ready-made hoi sin sauce in the supermarket and use it straight from the jar onto the rice roll (or pancake). In my version, sesame oil, dark soy and sugar (not healthy but allowed sometimes...) liven up the hoi sin and give it some depth. You will find wheatflour pancakes for Peking duck pancakes in Chinese supermarkets (usually in the freezer cabinets); they need steaming. I think rice paper rolls make for a delicious change, though, and these can be found on the shelf in oriental shops. Both pancakes and rice paper rolls can be stored easily, either in your store cupboard or freezer, and used when required.

Preparation time: **10 minutes plus marinating** Cooking time: **1 hour 30 minutes**

1. Place the duck on a rack over a roasting tin and pour over the boiling water. Discard the water and pat dry the duck with kitchen paper.
2. Mix together the ingredients for the glaze and brush over the duck, inside and out. Let it dry and glaze then brush again. Repeat, using most of the marinade but reserve 4–5 tablespoons. Ideally, allow the glaze to settle over the duck, leaving it uncovered in the fridge overnight.
3. Preheat the oven to 200°C/400°F/Gas Mark 6. Place the duck on a rack in a roasting tin. Transfer to the oven and cook for 45 minutes then turn over and brush the duck with the reserved marinade. Check that the bird is not getting too dark then cook for a further 45 minutes until the skin is crisp. Remove, cover, and let it rest.
4. To make the sauce, heat a pan or wok and add all the sauce ingredients except the blended cornflour. When the sauce starts to bubble slightly, add the cornflour and stir well. Set aside and let it cool.
5. Place some rice paper rolls in a bowl of hot water for less than 1 minute, remove and lay them on a plate to soften.
6. Carve and slice some duck. Place 1 teaspoon of sauce in the centre of a roll, add some duck, spring onions and cucumber, roll up and serve immediately.

# Sesame Prawn Toast

serves 2/makes 8

*1 teaspoon freshly grated ginger*
*1 large spring onion, finely chopped*
*1 egg white, beaten*
*1 tablespoon cornflour*
*dash of sesame oil*
*dash of soy sauce*
*8 tablespoons toasted sesame seeds*
*4 slices brown toast, halved, crusts removed*
*8 raw tiger prawns, shelled and deveined, tails on*
*2 pinches of salt*
*freshly ground black pepper*

*400ml groundnut oil*

This is a Chinese takeaway favourite; the crunchy sesame coating gives delicious flavour and texture to succulent tiger prawns. I love making original sesame prawn toast where the prawns are finely chopped, not minced, to give texture then spread onto slices of brown bread (a healthier option), sprinkled with plenty of sesame seeds, then fried until golden brown. Tired of making this over and over again in the same way, I decided to reinvent the recipe and keep the prawns whole to save time on the preparation.

**Preparation time: 15 minutes**     **Cooking time: 5 minutes**

**1.** Combine all the ingredients except the sesame seeds, toast and prawns in a shallow bowl. Put the sesame seeds into another bowl.

**2.** Dip each half piece of toast in the mixture and coat well. Then wrap the toast around a prawn and squeeze slightly so the bread fully covers the prawn. Roll the wrapped prawn in the sesame seeds and coat well. Repeat with the remaining prawns and pieces of toast.

**3.** Heat a wok over high heat, add the groundnut oil and shallow fry the sesame prawns until golden brown.

**4.** Drain the prawns on kitchen paper to remove the excess oil and serve immediately with Sweet Chilli Jam (see page 142).

# Beef and Chilli Bamboo Shoots in Little Gem Lettuce  serves 4

1 tablespoon groundnut oil

2 garlic cloves, crushed and finely chopped

1 tablespoon freshly grated ginger

1 medium red chilli, deseeded and finely chopped

200g minced beef (fine not coarse), seasoned
    with a pinch of cornflour, salt and ground
    white pepper

150g tinned stripped bamboo shoots, drained
    and finely diced

6 fresh shiitake mushrooms, sliced and
    finely diced

1 small shallot, finely chopped

2 tablespoons light soy sauce

dash of toasted sesame oil

1 large spring onion, finely chopped

1 small handful coriander, finely chopped

2 Little Gem lettuces, leaves separated
    and washed

50g ready roasted peanuts, finely chopped
    or ground

12–16 small mandarin segments, white
    membrane removed

I first sampled this delicious dish when I was 11 years old at a local Chinese restaurant in north London when my family was invited by my parents' new-found friends to celebrate our move to England from South Africa. My mother also fell in love with the dish and recreated it at home, serving it on iceberg lettuce. I remember her complaining about not being able to get fresh bamboo shoots (something she took for granted as my grandparents were farmers and had a bamboo farm), so she had to get used to buying the tinned variety.

I decided to reinvent and modernise this dish by adding small segments of mandarins and using Little Gem lettuce instead. This is a very happening dish – there is a real burst of flavours!

**Preparation time: 15 minutes**     **Cooking time: 10 minutes**

**1.** Heat a wok over high heat and add the oil.

**2.** Stir fry the garlic, ginger and red chilli for less than a minute. Add the seasoned minced beef and stir fry until it starts to turn brown. Throw in the bamboo shoots, mushrooms and shallot and stir fry for less than 1 minute. Season with soy sauce and sesame oil and stir well. Throw in the spring onion and coriander.

**3.** Arrange the lettuce leaves on a plate and divide the mixture among the leaves.

**4.** Sprinkle some roasted peanuts over each little parcel, add some mandarin segments to each one and serve.

# Chilli Spare Ribs   serves 2

1 teaspoon Chinese five-spice powder
1 tablespoon dark soy sauce
2 tablespoons shaosing rice wine or dry sherry
450g pork spare ribs
2 tablespoons potato flour
1 egg, beaten
2 medium red chillies, deseeded and
    finely chopped
400ml groundnut oil
1 teaspoon crushed dried chilli flakes (optional)
sea salt and ground white pepper

OK, this one is addictive and not ultra-healthy as it is fried but it is so tasty you can have it as a treat. If you don't want to fry the ribs, you can bake them, in which case you won't need the potato flour and egg mixture. Bake them in a preheated oven at 200°C/400°F/Gas Mark 6 for 25 minutes, put some sea salt, ground white pepper and chopped chillies in a small bowl and dip the ribs into the mix just before serving. Or just follow the recipe below – it's delicious either way.

Preparation time: **10 minutes plus marinating**
Cooking time: **15 minutes (25 minutes if baking)**

**1.** Put the five-spice powder, dark soy sauce and shaosing rice wine in a bowl. Marinate the ribs for as long as possible, overnight is best.

**2.** Mix together the potato flour and beaten egg.

**3.** Dip each spare rib in the mixture then roll it in the finely chopped chillies, coating it well. Repeat with all the ribs.

**4.** Heat a wok over high heat and add the oil. When a small piece of bread dropped into the oil turns golden brown in 15 seconds the oil is hot enough.

**5.** Deep fry the ribs until they have a crispy coating. You can sprinkle some dried chilli flakes over the ribs in the wok if you want a fiery kick.

**6.** Remove the ribs with a slotted spoon and drain any excess oil on kitchen paper.

**7.** Season with some sea salt and ground white pepper and serve immediately.

# Steamed Pork and Prawn Siu Mai Dumplings

serves 4/makes 16

for the filling

*200g pork mince*

*200g fresh raw prawns, shelled, deveined and*
*    finely chopped*

*1 large spring onion, finely chopped*

*1 tablespoon freshly grated ginger*

*1 tablespoon light soy sauce*

*1 tablespoon rice wine*

*1 teaspoon sesame oil*

*2 teaspoons cornflour*

*pinch of salt and ground black pepper*

*16 wonton wrappers (available in Chinese*
*    supermarkets)*

for the vinegar soy dressing

*2 tablespoons light soy sauce*

*2 tablespoons sesame oil*

*2 tablespoons rice vinegar (Chinese black rice*
*    vinegar is best)*

*1 teaspoon finely chopped coriander*

*1 teaspoon chillies, deseeded and finely chopped*

Siu Mai dumplings are pork and prawn bites enclosed in a wonton, and usually served in a bamboo basket. These open-wrapped parcels of deliciousness are a 'dim sum' favourite and very healthy too as they are steamed. (Dim sum is a real Chinese tradition that originated in the Canton (Guandong) province of China. Teahouses opened up to provide travellers on the Silk Road with teas and snacks served in bamboo baskets, giving them their 'yum-cha' break.) I first tried dim sum in Hong Kong when I was about 13. My father took my brother and me on a trip to visit my aunt. I remember being woken very early on a Sunday morning (suffering horrendously from jetlag) and taken to a bright colourful restaurant in Kowloon Bay. We must have arrived at 8 a.m. because, my aunt explained, we had to get there early to avoid the queues. The timing was perfect: soon after we arrived crowds of Hong Kong residents gathered. We proceeded to eat our way through plates and baskets full of delicacies wheeled to our table on trolleys. Being Taiwanese, I couldn't understand the waiters as they spoke only Cantonese but my aunt was very well versed and had everything under control. What a joyous breakfast and lunch it was – we didn't leave until noon! Whenever I make this recipe, it takes me back to Hong Kong.

Preparation time: **10 minutes**          Cooking time: **20 minutes**

**1.** Put all the filling ingredients in a bowl and mix thoroughly.

**2.** Take 2 teaspoons of the filling and place it in the centre of a wonton wrapper. Gather up the sides of the wrapper and mould around the filling in a ball shape, leaving the centre open. Make all the dumplings in this way.

**3.** Oil the bottom of a bamboo steamer. Fill a wok or pan with boiling water to a depth that will not submerge the base of the steamer. Place the steamer in the wok and steam for about 6–8 minutes.

**4.** Meanwhile, make the dressing by mixing together all the ingredients.

**5.** When the dumplings are cooked, serve with the dressing, or you could dip them in sweet chilli dipping sauce.

## Ching's extra tips:

**Fried Crispy Wontons:** Fill the wonton wrappers as before but gather all the corners into the middle of the wrapper and mould the wonton to enclose the filling completely. Then deep fry in a wok or pan of hot groundnut oil until golden brown and crispy. Drain on kitchen paper and serve.

**Wonton Noodle Soup:** Instead of deep frying, you can also place the whole complete wonton in 1 litre chicken stock with 200g chopped Chinese leaf, 2 tablespoons rice vinegar, 2 tablespoons light soy sauce and 2 finely chopped spring onions. Cook the wontons in the clear broth for 4–5 minutes. Sprinkle with coriander and serve.

# Five-a-Day Mixed Vegetable Stir Fry serves 2

2 tablespoons groundnut oil

2 garlic cloves, crushed and finely chopped

1 tablespoon freshly grated ginger

5 dried Chinese mushrooms, soaked in hot water
    for 20 minutes, finely chopped, stem discarded

1 carrot, sliced

1 red pepper, sliced

100g fresh baby corn, chopped into 1.5cm pieces

100g mangetout

100g cashew nuts

50ml vegetable stock

1 tablespoon oyster sauce

1 tablespoon light soy sauce

dash of sesame oil

1 tablespoon cornflour blended with 2 tablespoons
    cold water (optional)

1 spring onion, diagonally sliced

I find the two easiest ways to get my daily intake of a variety of vegetables is to make a salad or stir fry, and I'm a great fan of stir fries because they're served hot! You can vary the vegetables using whatever you have in your fridge. The key to a good stir fry is to ensure you don't overcook the vegetables by leaving them in the wok or pan too long, and you don't need a lot of oil. For tougher vegetables such as broccoli, you could add a sprinkle of water to help with the cooking process. As a general rule, always add the crunchier vegetables to the wok first and the softer ones last – that way all the vegetables still retain their 'bite'.

Preparation time: **10 minutes**          Cooking time: 10 minutes

**1.** Heat a wok over high heat and add the oil. Throw in the garlic and ginger. Cook for less than 1 minute then add the vegetables. Stir fry for less than 1 minute. Add the cashew nuts and stir fry for a further minute.

**2.** Add the vegetable stock, oyster sauce, light soy sauce and sesame oil.

**3.** Stir in the blended cornflour if you prefer a thicker sauce. Throw in the spring onion, give a final stir and then serve immediately with noodles or steamed rice.

# Egg, Leek and Potato and Noodle Stir Fry serves 2

3 tablespoons vegetable oil

2 eggs, beaten

1 potato, peeled and cut into thin julienne strips

1 leek, cut into thin julienne strips

200g cooked egg noodles

2 tablespoons oyster sauce

1 tablespoon light soy sauce

1/2 teaspoon sugar

2 spring onions, sliced diagonally

This is a simple but wholesome stir fry that is quick to make after a long day at work. It's one I discovered using leftover ingredients I had in the fridge, along with the help of a few essential store cupboard ingredients. The results are really satisfying. You can of course add more ingredients and, if you're a meat lover, some leftover roast pork would also make a wonderful combination.

Preparation time: **5 minutes**          Cooking time: **15 minutes**

**1.** Heat a wok over high heat and add 2 tablespoons of oil. Tip in the egg and swirl the pan to cook like a thin omelette until browned on both sides. Set aside to cool. Cut into strips.

**2.** Rinse out the wok with water and wipe with kitchen paper. Reheat the wok and add the remaining oil. Add the potato and stir fry for 9 minutes over high heat. Add a few drops of water to 'fire up' the wok then add the leek and stir for 1 minute. Add the cooked noodles, the oyster sauce, soy sauce and sugar. Stir fry well then add the spring onions.

**3.** Add the omelette strips back into the wok, mix well and serve immediately.

# Hot Chilli Prawns on Yellow Shi Noodles   serves 2

150g dried yellow shi noodles or other
    wheatflour noodles
2 tablespoons olive oil, plus extra for drizzling
6 large garlic cloves, crushed and chopped
1 tablespoon freshly grated ginger
3 medium red chillies, deseeded and chopped
300g fresh raw tiger prawns, shelled and deveined
    (tail on or off, optional)
100ml boiling water
1 tablespoon lime juice
2 spring onions, chopped lengthways
4 tablespoons freshly chopped coriander, stalks
    and leaves

for the sauce
200ml boiling water
5 tablespoons ketchup
2 tablespoons light soy sauce
1 tablespoon soft brown sugar
2 teaspoons cornflour

This is one of my favourite wok dishes: fast and simple but truly delish! The flavours are spicy, sweet and delicately tangy. To create the sweetness, I use tomato ketchup which gives great colour too – it's a really versatile store cupboard ingredient. You could also make it a seafood medley by adding scallops and squid, served over steamed Thai rice or crispy pan-fried noodles. Shi noodles are a great accompaniment. They are wheatflour noodles, thinner than spaghetti, and they absorb the flavours of the sauce really well. Do make sure you serve this dish instantly, otherwise the herbs start to wilt!

**Preparation time: 15 minutes**      **Cooking time: 10 minutes**

**1.** Prepare the noodles according to the instructions on the packet, drain and immediately refresh under cold running water to rinse away the starch and keep them springy. Set aside.

**2.** Mix all the ingredients for the sauce and set aside.

**3.** Heat a wok over high heat and add the olive oil. Add the garlic, ginger and chillies, stir fry for a few seconds then add the prawns and stir fry until they start to go pink.

**4.** Stir in the sauce ingredients and cook for less than 1 minute, then add the 100ml boiling water, the lime juice, spring onions and coriander.

**5.** Refresh the prepared noodles under boiling water, then drizzle with some olive oil and divide between 2 bowls. Place the prawns and sauce on top and serve immediately.

# Lemon Monkfish serves 2

2 x 150g monkfish fillets
½ teaspoon salt
½ teaspoon ground white pepper
1 tablespoon cornflour
1 tablespoon groundnut oil

for the lemon sauce
juice of 1 lemon
300ml vegetable stock
2 tablespoons clear honey
2 tablespoons light brown sugar
1 tablespoon cornflour blended with 1 teaspoon
    cold water

to garnish
2 lemon slices
1 spring onion, green ends only, finely chopped

You can use any firm white fish in this dish, cod or halibut are just as good as monkfish. Whatever you choose, make sure that the fish does not smell and that the flesh is firm and not too soft to touch. The gills should be blood red and the eyes should shine and not be glazed. If you can get to the local fishmonger, even better, that way you can see the whole fish – and often get a wider selection. This is a simple light main course, delicious served with steamed jasmine rice and Chinese greens such as gai lan (Chinese broccoli) or pak choy, but it's good with French beans too. You could also adapt this recipe and use chicken breast instead.

Preparation time: **10 minutes**      Cooking time: **10 minutes**

**1.** Wash the monkfish and pat dry with kitchen paper. Season with the salt and ground white pepper and dust lightly with cornflour.

**2.** Heat a wok or pan over high heat and add the oil. Fry the monkfish until lightly browned then turn over using a pair of chopsticks or a pallet knife and brown the other side. Transfer to a plate or small flat dish, cover with foil, and keep warm in the oven.

**3.** Put the lemon juice, vegetable stock, honey and sugar in a small pan and bring to the boil. Stir in the blended cornflour to thicken the sauce.

**4.** Pour a generous serving of the lemon sauce over the fish. Garnish with thinly sliced lemon, sprinkle with spring onions and serve.

# Chilli and Pepper Squid serves 2

200g fresh squid, washed and cleaned,
   cut into rings
1 egg, beaten
1/2 teaspoon sea salt
1/2 teaspoon ground white pepper
4 tablespoons potato flour
200ml groundnut oil

to serve
100g iceberg lettuce, shredded
100g carrots, cut into fine strips
1 spring onion, chopped lengthways
2 red chillies, deseeded and chopped into rings
small handful of coriander, chopped, stalks
   and leaves

This dish makes my mouth water even thinking about it. If you are not a fan of squid, this dish just might convert you. Squid rings are dusted with potato flour, seasoned with sea salt and ground white pepper and then shallow fried to give a crispy coating. You can also use frozen squid rings, but fresh are best. Served on a bed of shredded iceberg lettuce and finely stripped carrots with a generous sprinkling of fresh red chillies, spring onions and fresh coriander, this makes a great starter or shared main.

Preparation time: **15 minutes**          Cooking time: **10 minutes**

**1.** Coat the squid with the beaten egg. Season with salt and pepper then dust generously with potato flour, coating each ring well.
**2.** Heat the oil in a deep-fat fryer or wok to 180°C/350°F, or until a tiny piece of bread browns in 15 seconds. Be particularly careful if deep frying in a wok.
**3.** Add the squid rings and fry until golden brown then drain any excess oil on kitchen paper.
**4.** Serve on iceberg lettuce and carrots, sprinkled with generous amounts of spring onion, chillies and coriander.

# Sichuan Pepper Prawns serves 4 as a main or 6 as a starter with other dishes

1 tablespoon olive oil
400g fresh tiger prawns, head off, deveined
   but shell on
sea salt and Sichuan peppercorns

Mmmm... stir-fried tiger prawns coated in cracked Sichuan pepper and sea salt. This is a dish to be shared at the table. You must use your fingers when eating this one as the flavour is on the shell of the prawns and by picking up the prawns to shell them, those flavours transfer to your fingers – finger-lickin' good! I sometimes vary the eating technique – simply hold the prawns to your mouth and using your teeth and starting from the end, squeeze the succulent prawn away from the shell... delightful.

Preparation time: **10 minutes**          Cooking time: **5 minutes**

**1.** Heat a wok over high heat and add the oil.
**2.** Crack and crush some Sichuan peppercorns with a pestle and mortar or spice grinder.
**3.** Add the prawns to the wok and stir fry until they turn pink and the shells start to brown slightly. Season the prawns very well with sea salt and the cracked Sichuan pepper. Stir well and serve immediately.

# Scallops in Chilli Black Bean Sauce on Gai Lan with Enoki Mushrooms serves 4

1 tablespoon groundnut oil

1 garlic clove, crushed and finely chopped

1 teaspoon freshly grated ginger

2 tablespoons black beans, soaked in shaosing
  rice wine, crushed

12 large scallops, coral removed if preferred

2 teaspoons oyster sauce

100ml green tea

2 medium red chillies, deseeded and chopped

dash of light soy sauce

1½ tablespoons cornflour blended with
  2 tablespoons cold water

2 spring onions, diagonally sliced

200g gai lan (Chinese broccoli) or baby
  asparagus

100g enoki mushrooms

There's nothing quite like homemade black bean sauce. I think fermented, salted black beans should be sold in all supermarkets. These pungent beans have been cooked in salt so you need to rinse them in cold water to remove the excess salt. For extra flavour, put some in a jar and pour in enough shaosing rice wine to cover the beans – this way they keep in your condiments cupboard for months. To use, spoon straight from the jar – beans and wine. Together they make a tasty pair.

Preparation time: **10 minutes**       Cooking time: **10 minutes**

1. Fill a wok or pan with boiling water to a depth that will not immerse the base of the steamer. Place the gai lan in the steamer and steam for 3–4 minutes. Remove the steamer from the wok and set aside, covered, to keep warm.

2. Heat a wok or pan over high heat and add the oil. Throw in the garlic, ginger and the black beans and stir fry for less than 1 minute. Add the scallops and stir fry for less than 1 minute. They will start to turn a more opaque white when cooked. Add the oyster sauce and green tea and stir fry for 1–2 minutes then throw in the chillies and season with the light soy sauce.

3. When the scallops turn completely opaque, stir in the blended cornflour then sprinkle in the spring onions.

4. Arrange the steamed vegetables on a serving plate, top with the raw mushrooms, scallops, and pour plenty of the spicy sauce on top and serve. You can also serve this with Jasmine Rice (see page 142).

# Bacon and Egg-fried Rice   serves 2

1 tablespoon vegetable oil

2 eggs, beaten

80g unsmoked streaky bacon rashers, chopped
    into small dice

70g frozen peas

300g cooked cold rice

2 tablespoons light soy sauce

1 tablespoon sesame oil

ground white pepper

I cannot function without a good hearty breakfast. This recipe is one that I usually make from leftover rice I have in the fridge and of course I always keep a packet of garden peas in the freezer for when I'm in need of making a quick fix like egg-fried rice. This has become one of my favourite breakfasts, washed down with a glass of freshly squeezed orange juice. Naughty but good.

Preparation time: **5 minutes**          Cooking time: **5 minutes**

**1.** Heat a wok over high heat and add the vegetable oil. Tip the beaten eggs into the wok, stir to scramble, then remove and set aside.

**2.** Put the bacon into the same wok and stir fry until browned and slightly crispy.

**3.** Throw in the frozen peas and stir fry for less than a minute. Add the rice and mix well until the rice has broken down.

**4.** Add the egg back into the wok and stir through. Season with light soy sauce, sesame oil and a pinch of ground white pepper and serve immediately.

# Nutty Chicken Cool Noodle Salad  serves 2 as a main or 4 as a starter

*400g dried wholewheat flour noodles*

*toasted sesame oil for drizzling*

*½ cucumber, cored and cut into long strips*
*(ideally using a mandolin)*

*1 large carrot, cut into long strips (ideally using*
*a mandolin)*

*1 yellow pepper, deseeded and cut into strips*

*1 mango, peeled, stoned and cut into strips*

*1 spring onion cut into long thin strips*

*350g cooked skinless chicken breast, shredded*


*for the peanut dressing*

*6 tablespoons olive oil*

*1 tablespoon sesame oil*

*1 garlic clove, crushed and finely chopped*

*1 tablespoon minced ginger*

*1 red chilli, deseeded and chopped*

*2 tablespoons light soy sauce*

*2 tablespoons rice vinegar*

*3 tablespoons crunchy peanut butter*

*1 teaspoon brown sugar*

*juice of 1½ lemons*


*handful of chopped roasted peanuts (optional)*

My family have been eating this recipe for years. However, it was only a few years ago when I started my food business and came across a similar recipe in a food magazine that I realised everyone calls this recipe Bang Bang Chicken! In Taiwan, in the summertime, we have Hua Sheng Liang Mein which roughly translates as 'nutty cool noodle'. It is an irresistible noodle salad snack made with shredded chicken breast, cucumber slices, springy wheatflour noodles and delicious peanut dressing. I'm not surprised this dish made it to Taiwan. Bang Bang Chicken originated in the Sichuan province in China, and Sichuanese cuisine (which is predominantly hot and spicy) has a great influence on Taiwanese cuisine. The nation certainly has a taste for chillies! However, if you are not a fan, adjust the amount of chilli to your liking.

I think my family recipe in this case could serve as a modern take on Bang Bang Chicken and my version is served with tangy mango slices. I present my Nutty Chicken Cool Noodle Salad – refreshing on a hot summer's day.

Preparation time: **10 minutes plus refrigerating**
Cooking time: **30 minutes**

**1.** Cook the noodles according to the packet instructions, then drain and rinse in cold water. Drizzle with a few dashes of sesame oil to keep them from sticking together. Place on a plate and cover with clingfilm and chill in the fridge while you slice and prepare the rest.

**2.** In serving bowls, place equal amounts of cooked noodles. Then add layers of cucumber strips, carrots strips, yellow pepper, mango slices, spring onion strips and shredded chicken. Cover with clingfilm and refrigerate for 30 minutes. This salad tastes refreshing when cold so refrigeration is a must.

**3.** When ready to serve, whizz all the dressing ingredients in a blender and pour a generous amount over the salad. For an even nuttier flavour and added crunch, sprinkle some chopped roasted peanuts over the top. Enjoy with chilled Chinese beer.

# Char Siu Pork on Steamed Pak Choy
# with Sweet Orange Sauce  serves 2 as a main or 4 as a starter

1 x 500g pork fillet
400g pak choy

for the marinade
2 garlic cloves, crushed and finely chopped
2 tablespoons freshly grated ginger
50ml light soy sauce
50ml rice wine
3 tablespoons brown sugar
1 tablespoon hoi sin sauce
2 tablespoons yellow bean sauce
1 tablespoon vegetable oil
60ml honey
salt and freshly ground black pepper

for the sweet orange sauce
juice of 3 oranges
dash of light soy sauce
3 tablespoons honey
pinch of cinnamon
1 tablespoon cornflour blended with 2 tablespoons
    cold water

1 spring onion, finely sliced

I have to thank David Wong, a great friend and excellent Chinese chef, for giving me his scrumptious Char Siu pork recipe. Char Siu is usually served with soy sauce gravy over steamed Chinese leaf with plain white rice. But I have adapted it. The orange sauce was born when I overcooked the Char Siu, which became too dry, then I ran out of soy sauce so I had to improvise with oranges instead and what I had in the store cupboard. Thankfully, it worked deliciously well and saved the dish! This recipe can be served as a main or shared to make 4 mini starters.

Preparation time: **10 minutes plus marinating**     Cooking time: **40 minutes**

**1.** Cut slashes into the sides of the pork fillet.
**2.** Combine all the marinade ingredients and marinate the fillet for as long as possible, overnight is best.
**3.** Preheat the oven to 200°C/400°F/Gas Mark 6.
**4.** Remove the pork from the marinade, place on a rack over a roasting tray and pour hot water into the tray to half fill the tray. Roast the pork for 20 minutes then turn the fillet over and brush with the remaining marinade, basting well. Reduce the temperature to 180°C/350°F/Gas Mark 4 and roast for a further 20 minutes. Cover with foil and keep warm in the oven.
**5.** Fill a wok or pan with boiling water to a depth that will not submerge the base of the steamer. Place the pak choy in the steamer and steam for less than 2 minutes.
**6.** Heat the orange juice, soy sauce, honey and cinnamon in a small pan. When the sauce boils, stir in the blended cornflour and remove from the heat.
**7.** Slice the pork, arrange on the pak choy and drizzle the sweet orange sauce over the top. Sprinkle with freshly chopped spring onion and serve with Egg-fried Rice (see page 142).

# Kung Po Chicken serves 4

340g skinless chicken breast, sliced then diced
1 tablespoon cornflour
$^1/_2$ teaspoon salt
$^1/_2$ teaspoon ground Sichuan peppercorns

for the sauce
2 tablespoons rice vinegar
2 tablespoons hoi sin sauce
1 tablespoon dark soy sauce
$^1/_2$ teaspoon crushed dried chilli flakes

1 tablespoon groundnut oil
1 medium chilli, deseeded and chopped
1 onion, peeled and chopped
1 green pepper, deseeded and chopped
    into chunks
6 baby corn, chopped into 1cm slices

This one delivers a taste sensation that is irresistible for those who love heat. But it isn't only heat that you detect; there are sweet, tangy and savoury elements too. The recipe is another one originating from Sichuan province in China, a region that has a love of chillies. I have served this dish countless times at dinner parties and it always gets the thumbs up. You can also use prawns instead of chicken.

Preparation time: **10 minutes**    Cooking time: **10 minutes**

**1.** Mix all the sauce ingredients in a bowl.
**2.** Heat a wok over high heat and add the groundnut oil. Season the chicken with the cornflour, salt and Sichuan pepper. Throw into the wok and stir fry the chicken for about 6 minutes until golden brown. Remove and set aside.
**3.** Throw all the vegetables into the wok and stir fry until al dente. Throw the chicken back into the wok, add the sauce and stir well. Serve with Jasmine Rice (see page 142).

# Chicken Curry Sauce with Spring Onion Flatbread  serves 2

for the chicken

*2 tablespoons groundnut oil*

*400g skinless chicken breast*

*2 pinches of salt*

*¹/₂ teaspoon ground white pepper*

*1 tablespoon cornflour*

for the curry sauce

*1 tablespoon groundnut oil*

*1 garlic clove, crushed and finely chopped*

*1 tablespoon freshly grated ginger*

*1 green chilli, deseeded and finely chopped*

*1 onion, sliced into crescent moon shapes*

*1 small carrot, sliced diagonally*

*1 handful broccoli flowers*

*500ml chicken stock*

*2 star anise, whole*

*1 teaspoon turmeric*

*¹/₂–1 teaspoon Madras hot curry powder*
    *(according to taste)*

*1 tablespoon brown sugar*

*1 tablespoon cornflour blended with 2 tablespoons*
    *cold water*

*1 spring onion, finely chopped*

for the flatbread (makes 4 large ones)

*130g plain flour plus extra for kneading*

*2 pinches of salt*

*110ml hot water*

*dab of olive oil*

*1¹/₂ tablespoons toasted sesame oil*

*1 spring onion, finely chopped*

This recipe reminds me of the comforting curry from my local Chinese takeaway. Mild and sweet, it's great on a Friday night with some Chinese beers, a good DVD and your loved one to share it with. I had to experiment a few times to get the flavours right. The secret is adding star anise – it gives the curry a gorgeous aroma. If you're feeling lazy, forget the flatbread, and serve it with some rice or try my easy Coriander Couscous recipe on page 149. I do, however, like to cook the chicken separately as I think that way it has more flavour, and adding it to the curry at the last moment ensures that its flavour isn't lost in the sauce. Then again, if you're pushed for time, just throw in the chicken pieces after the ginger in step 2 below. Who says only Indians do good curries?

Preparation time: **12 minutes**      Cooking time: **50 minutes**

**1.** Heat a wok over high heat and add the oil. Season the chicken breasts with the salt, pepper and cornflour. Throw into the wok and stir fry until golden brown, about 6 minutes. Remove and set aside.

**2.** Rinse out the wok and reheat (or use a separate small pan). Add the oil then throw in the garlic, ginger and chilli and stir fry for less than 1 minute. Then add the onion and stir fry for less than 1 minute until browned. Throw in the carrot and broccoli flowers and stir fry for less than 1 minute.

**3.** Add the chicken stock, star anise, turmeric, curry powder and brown sugar and bring to the boil. Add the blended cornflour and stir well. Transfer the curry sauce to a heatproof dish, cover with foil and place in the oven at 150°C/300°F/Gas Mark 3 while you make the flatbread.

**4.** For the flatbread, combine the flour and salt in a bowl, stir in the hot water and work into a dough. Turn out onto a floured surface and knead for 5 minutes until the dough is smooth and elastic. Oil the surface with a little olive oil. Place in a floured bowl and cover with a damp tea towel and let it rest at room temperature for 20 minutes.

**5.** Take the dough, roll into a long sausage then divide into 4 equal pieces. Roll each piece into a ball using the palm of your hand and then flatten out with a rolling pin into a small disc. Brush with sesame oil and sprinkle some finely chopped spring onion onto each disc. Reform them into balls again then roll into flat discs about 3mm thick.

**6.** Heat a wok or pan over high heat and add 1 tablespoon olive oil (no need to use any oil if you have a non-stick pan, just dry heat it). Heat the discs until golden brown, turning them over to cook them on both sides. Keep each one warm, covered with foil, while you make the rest.

**7.** When ready to serve, add the chicken pieces to the curry sauce and allow to heat through, garnish with spring onion and serve with the flatbread.

# Sichuan Pepper Beef with Five-a-day Vegetables and Five-spice Gravy

serves 2

2 sirloin steaks, cut into strips

2 tablespoons groundnut oil
1 medium red chilli, deseeded and chopped
½ onion, chopped
1 small handful broccoli
1 small handful chopped mangetout
1 small handful chopped carrots
1 small handful chopped baby corn
300ml hot fresh beef or vegetable stock
1 tablespoon light soy sauce
1 tablespoon cornflour blended with 2 tablespoons
    cold water
1 spring onion, finely sliced
salt and ground white pepper

for the marinade
1 tablespoon shaosing rice wine or dry sherry
2 teaspoons ground Sichuan pepper
1 teaspoon dark soy sauce
½ teaspoon Chinese five-spice powder
2 garlic cloves, crushed and finely chopped

This makes for a fast, easy and delicious supper. I love rustling up this one because it's a real comfort dish for me. Chinese five-spice is the key to this recipe as it flavours the gravy beautifully. This is a real balanced meal of protein and vegetables and the method of cooking used is a 'saucy' stir fry, which makes it really healthy too as the vegetables are al dente, retaining their nutrients. Serve with generous helpings of plain steamed jasmine rice to soak up the yummy gravy.

Preparation time: **10 minutes, plus marinating**     Cooking time: **20 minutes**

**1.** Mix all the marinade ingredients in a bowl and marinate the beef for as long as possible, overnight is best.
**2.** Heat a wok over high heat and add the oil. Stir-fry the marinated beef for 2 minutes.
**3.** Add the red chilli and onion and stir fry for less than 1 minute then add the rest of the vegetables and stir fry for 1 minute.
**4.** Add the stock (it needs to be hot) and mix well. Season with light soy sauce. Bring to the boil, add the blended cornflour and stir well.
**5.** Add the spring onion, season to taste and serve with Jasmine Rice (see page 142).

# Mango Pudding serves 4

450g fresh mangoes (peeled and stoned weight)
200ml evaporated milk
100g caster sugar
200ml water
22g powdered gelatine (2 sachets)

to decorate
juice and zest of 1 lime
icing sugar for dusting
sprigs of mint

This one is a real delight: simple to make, and it can be made well ahead. Zesty and fruity – it's perfect for children too. Definitely one of my all-time favourites.

Preparation time: **10 minutes**     Chilling time: **1 hour**

**1.** Purée the prepared mangoes in a blender. Transfer to a bowl. Pour the evaporated milk onto the mango purée, add the sugar and mix well.

**2.** In a measuring jug, measure 200ml hot water and add the gelatine (and not the other way round or you will get lumpy bits.) Quickly stir until all the gelatine granules have dissolved then add to the puréed mangoes and mix well.

**3.** Ladle the mixture into 4 dishes. Place on a tray and refrigerate for at least 1 hour.

**4.** When ready to serve, briefly put the dishes in a baking tray with some hot water to help loosen the pudding. Use a flat knife to run round the edges of the pudding, place a plate on top of the dish and quickly invert it – the pudding should fall onto the plate. Squeeze over some lime juice, dust with icing sugar and decorate with lime zest and a sprig of mint.

# Banana Pancakes and Fresh Strawberries serves 4

2 tablespoons lemon juice
45g caster sugar
2 tablespoons Grand Marnier
4 firm bananas, sliced

340g plain flour, sifted with a pinch of salt
2 tablespoons caster sugar
1 teaspoon baking powder
1 tablespoon butter
2 eggs, separated
180ml whole milk
1 teaspoon vanilla essence
4 tablespoons groundnut oil

to serve
fresh strawberries
Lychee and Vanilla Ice Cream (see opposite)
icing sugar for dusting

My recipe is a cross between a pancake and a fritter in which whole pieces of banana would be dipped into the mixture then deep-fried. I prefer the lighter pancake version below. There is a fair number of ingredients but most you'll have in your store cupboard. Give these pancakes a try: definitely worth it.

Preparation: **15 minutes**     Cooking time: **10 minutes**

**1.** Mix the lemon juice, caster sugar and Grand Marnier in a bowl and toss the bananas in it.

**2.** Mix the flour, salt, sugar and baking powder in a bowl.

**3.** In a third bowl, melt the butter in a microwave, then mix in the egg yolks, milk and vanilla.

**4.** Lift the bananas from the marinade, set aside, and stir the marinade into the egg mixture. Add this combined mixture to the dry flour mix and mix into a pancake batter. Beat the egg whites until stiff and gently fold into the batter.

**5.** Heat a flat-based heavy pan over high heat and add the groundnut oil. Ladle in a quarter of the pancake mixture and cook like an omelette. Place banana slices on the surface, as if decorating a pizza! After 1 minute, when the underside is brown, flip the pancake over. Remove and keep warm while you make 3 more pancakes in the same way.

**6.** Serve with strawberries, ice cream and a little icing sugar. Single cream is extra naughty…

# Lychee and Vanilla Ice Cream   serves 4

*900ml double cream*
*150g caster sugar (or according to taste)*
*1 teaspoon vanilla extract*
*2 vanilla pods*
*1 x 340g tin of lychees, whizzed in a blender*
    *with their syrup*
*sprigs of mint to decorate*

When I was growing up in Taiwan I was addicted to lychees but my mother would never allow me to eat too many. The Chinese believe that every food has a 'yin–yang' quality and some are 'heat-giving' foods and others 'cooling'. This applies to the cooking techniques as well as the ingredients. For example, deep-frying gives food a 'yang' heat-giving quality whereas steaming is neutral, and raw foods are cooling or 'yin'. As a child I was never allowed too much of any one type of food, always striving to achieve a balance in what I ate. Both lychees and ice-cream are considered 'yang' foods so this is my naughty 'yang–yang' lychee and vanilla ice-cream which my mother would disapprove of. However, I think never in excess is always OK! I like to make a huge tub of this and store it in the freezer as an accompaniment to other desserts or to enjoy just on its own.

Preparation time: **5 minutes**          Cooking time: **5 minutes**
Freezing time: **between 25 minutes and 5 hours depending on method**

**1.** Pour the double cream into a pan. Add the caster sugar and vanilla extract (much better than vanilla 'flavouring') and heat gently to dissolve the sugar.

**2.** Slice the vanilla pods down the length of the pod, scrape out the sticky seeds with the tip of a knife and add them to the pan. (Keep the vanilla pods in a jar of sugar to make it fragrant.) Add the blitzed lychees. Give the mixture a good stir until the sugar has dissolved. Then leave it to cool.

**3.** The mixture is then ready to pour into an ice-cream machine. Follow the manufacturer's instructions to churn the mixture. If you don't have a machine, transfer the mixture to a freezerproof bowl, cover and freeze for 2–3 hours until just frozen. Then, using a fork or whisk, break up any ice crystals. Return it to the freezer for a further 2 hours, break up the ice again, then refreeze until solid. Just before serving, transfer it to the fridge to allow it to soften a little.

**4.** Serve decorated with mint sprigs.

# Chocolate Sesame Balls  serves 4/makes 12 balls

300g glutinous rice flour
65g soft brown sugar dissolved in 100ml boiling
   water in a jug
100ml cold water
100g dark chocolate (70% cocoa solids), broken
   into 24 pieces
80g white sesame seeds
650ml oil for deep frying

to serve
100g dark chocolate (70% cocoa solids)
strawberries or cape gooseberries (optional)

Ooh la la! These are what I call my naughty but nice Chinese-style profiteroles. In this recipe, glutinous rice flour is used to make a snug casing for pieces of dark chocolate moulded into a ball shape. The balls are coated in fragrant sesame seeds and then deep-fried. They expand and turn golden brown and the sesame seeds toast in the oil, giving a crunchy outer crust. Meanwhile, the chocolate inside has melted. And if that's not enough my friends, melted chocolate is poured over – the ultimate grand finale! For chocolate lovers, this is a must-try recipe. So, forget the traditional Chinese red bean paste filling and hands up for dark chocolate.

Preparation time: **15 minutes**    Cooking time: **10 minutes**

**1.** Put the rice flour into a bowl and make a well in the centre.
**2.** Stir the sugar and water to ensure it has dissolved. Pour it into the flour and add the cold water. Combine to make a dough and knead for 5 minutes into a ball.
**3.** Dust your hands with some rice flour and shape the dough into 12 balls roughly the size of golf balls.
**4.** Holding a dough ball in one hand, use the thumb of the other and make a hole into the dough to form a cup. Press 2 pieces of chocolate, one on top of the other, into the hole and gather the edges of the dough together to encase the chocolate completely. Do this with all the dough, then roll each of the balls in your hands until perfectly round, then roll them in the sesame seeds.
**5.** In a double boiler or a heatproof bowl set over a pan of barely simmering water, break up the second bar of chocolate and stir with a wooden spoon until it starts to melt. Once melted do not stir again but leave it over the hot water until you are ready to serve.
**6.** Heat the oil in a deep-fat fryer or wok to 180°C/350°F, or until a tiny piece of the dough browns in 15 seconds. Be particularly careful if deep frying in a wok. Deep fry the sesame seed balls, a few at a time, until the sesame seeds turn golden brown and the balls start to float to the surface, approximately 3–4 minutes.
**7.** Once cooked, place the sesame balls on a tray lined with kitchen paper to drain off excess oil while you cook the remainder. Serve warm, with the melted chocolate poured over. If you wish, you can cut open one of the balls on each serving and place a strawberry or cape gooseberry in the bed of chocolate.

# 2. Traditional Home Cooking

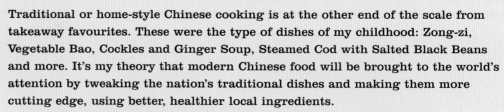

Traditional or home-style Chinese cooking is at the other end of the scale from takeaway favourites. These were the type of dishes of my childhood: Zong-zi, Vegetable Bao, Cockles and Ginger Soup, Steamed Cod with Salted Black Beans and more. It's my theory that modern Chinese food will be brought to the world's attention by tweaking the nation's traditional dishes and making them more cutting edge, using better, healthier local ingredients.

Chinese cooking is traditionally based on Chinese medicine and the philosophy behind our cuisine is about health and balance. These values echo the principles of yin and yang: we balance these forces by nourishing the body with foods that are 'cooling' and others that are 'heat-giving'. The Chinese dietary tradition focuses on eating to harmonise with the season. So in autumn we prepare the body for the cold months and provide fuel by eating grains, nuts, seeds and squashes. In winter most meat, nourishing soups and congee are served. In spring cooling foods such as leafy greens and sprouts rejuvenate the body, while in summer citrus fruits, melons, leafy greens, mung and soy beans are a must. The cooking technique of food also contributes a cooling or heat-giving quality. For example, steaming, boiling and stir frying are 'neutral', salads are cooling while braising and deep frying are 'heat giving'. However, ingredients are key too, because you can warm the food by adding heat-inducing garlic, ginger or chillies.

My grandmother taught me the yin–yang principle. She also used to lecture me on the importance of balancing the textures of soft, crunchy and chewy. Chinese cooks always try to incorporate at least two textures in any one dish. These should be set against a balance of flavours including at least two or three of the basic five: salty, sour, sweet, bitter and fiery. All these influences have inspired the recipes in this chapter and I am proud to include some of my grandmother's and to keep her culinary traditions alive.

My hope is that Chinese takeaway menus will no longer be confined to 'sweet and sour' when there is so much more to offer. Restaurants tend to have two menus, one for western palates and one for eastern palates; I would like to see them combined as one that caters for both. Chinese restaurateurs should provide food they are proud of. After all, being true to one's culinary heritage and sharing it with the world has to be a good thing.

# Once-a-month Savoury–Sour Vegetarian

# Noodle Soup serves 4 as a main or 6 as a starter

1 litre vegetable stock
1 tablespoon freshly grated ginger
1/2 Chinese leaf, chopped into 2cm strips
small handful of woodear mushrooms,
    soaked in boiling water for 20 minutes,
    chopped into long strips
3 dried Chinese mushrooms, soaked in
    boiling water for 20 minutes, chopped into
    long strips, stalks discarded
1 small tin of bamboo shoots, cut into long strips
1 small pack of mung bean noodles
1 small block fresh tofu, cut into long strips
2 tablespoons light soy sauce
2 tablespoons rice vinegar
1 egg, whisked (optional)
1 red chilli, deseeded and chopped (optional)
salt and freshly ground black pepper

1 spring onion, finely chopped
small handful of coriander, finely chopped

On the fifteenth of every month in the lunar calendar, when the moon is full and at its roundest, my family has a tradition of being vegetarian. This tradition originated from my grandmother, a devout Buddhist. She and many of the faith believe that if you are Buddhist and not completely vegetarian, it is important to give up meat for one day of the month to reconnect with the ideal behind Buddhism, which is to be compassionate to all living beings including animals. This is our family vegetarian recipe. It is a clear soup broth made with lots of Chinese leaf, crunchy woodear mushrooms, earthy Chinese mushrooms, bamboo shoots and fresh beancurd (dofu or tofu) combined with clear mung bean noodles in a seasoned savoury and sour broth. It is much like the hot and sour soup or Suan La Tang served in Chinese restaurants. Add a chilli or two if you wish.

Preparation time: **20 minutes**          Cooking time: **20 minutes**

**1.** Heat the stock in a large pan to simmering point and add the ginger, Chinese leaf, woodear mushrooms, Chinese mushrooms and bamboo shoots. Gently stir and cook for 5 minutes. Add the mung bean noodles, cook for 1 further minute, then add the tofu. Season to taste with the light soy sauce, rice vinegar, salt and pepper and bring to the boil. Add the beaten egg and chilli, if using.

**2.** Sprinkle with some spring onion and coriander and serve in large noodle bowls.

# Steamed Egg with Scallops, Chinese Mushroom and Caviar   serves 2

4 eggs, beaten

4 fresh prepared scallops, corals removed
   if preferred

1 teaspoon freshly grated ginger

1 dried Chinese mushroom, pre-soaked for
   20 minutes in boiling water, stalk discarded,
   finely chopped

1 small spring onion, finely chopped

2 tablespoons finely chopped coriander

1 teaspoon sesame oil

1 teaspoon light soy sauce

salt and freshly ground black pepper

to garnish

2 teaspoons caviar (or salmon fish roe from
   oriental stores)

4 chives, finely chopped

How else can you serve eggs apart from fried, scrambled, baked, poached and boiled? Steaming eggs is a breath of fresh air but it's not a new method – my mother has been cooking eggs in this way since I was a baby. She found it an easy way of giving her children nutritious food that was neither difficult to digest nor eat. There are many variations: another home favourite of mine is to add dried Chinese shrimps, scallops and nori (Japanese seaweed) to the beaten egg mixture. The sweet scallops combined with the tender egg and smoky Chinese mushrooms make this particular recipe a winner. It always goes down well at a dinner party as it uses extravagant ingredients such as scallops and caviar, but be warned: you can only fit 2 servings into a bamboo steamer at once so you have to double up on the number of steamers according to the number of guests.

Preparation time: **20 minutes**        Cooking time: **15 minutes**

**1.** Mix all the ingredients in a bowl except the garnish.

**2.** Divide the mixture between 2 Chinese ceramic bowls with lids.

**3.** Put 1.5 litres water into a wok over high heat. Place the bowls in a bamboo steamer and put the steamer into the wok, making sure the base is not submerged. Steam for 15 minutes. To check the egg is cooked, run a toothpick through the centre – it should come out clean.

**4.** Spoon 1 teaspoon of caviar and the chopped chives over each bowl and serve.

# Cockles and Ginger Soup serves 4

700ml boiling water
200g fresh cockles, shells washed
4cm piece ginger root, peeled, cut into matchsticks
handful of coriander, stems and leaves,
    roughly chopped
salt and ground white pepper

This simple cleansing recipe is my grandmother's. It was she who introduced me, aged five, to all the culinary delights of homemade Chinese food. She loved to cook us a feast and she would send my grandfather on his moped to the local market to select the freshest ingredients. My grandfather, moaning and cursing, would go off, but we all think he secretly enjoyed it. He was known to the local farmers and traders and always came home boasting that he'd struck a bargain!

This one doesn't require much seasoning; the cockles provide sweetness and the ginger gives a little heat. Salt, pepper and plenty of coriander is just enough.

Preparation time: **5 minutes**          Cooking time: **8 minutes**

**1.** Heat a pan over high heat, fill with boiling water from the kettle and bring to the boil. Add the cockles and ginger and cook until all the shells are open.
**2.** Season the soup with a pinch of salt and pepper. Sprinkle in the coriander and serve.

# Mother's Tomato and Egg Clear Soup with Seaweed serves 2

3 ripe tomatoes
500ml vegetable stock, simmering
2 eggs, whisked
dash of light soy sauce
dash of sesame oil
pinch of freshly ground black pepper
1 tablespoon cornflour blended with 2 tablespoons
    cold water
1 sheet nori (dried seaweed)
1 spring onion

My friends tell me that when they felt poorly they would be tucked up in bed after a bowl of their mother's homemade chicken soup. In my home, it was steaming bowlfuls of my mother's tomato and egg soup that did the job every time. She would skin the tomatoes first (though this is optional), before adding them to simmering vegetable stock, then pour in beaten eggs, lightly stirring, to make a beautiful web-like pattern. She would season it with light soy and fragrant toasted sesame oil then break up a few dried sheets of seaweed (nori, which is used to make sushi), and throw them in for a few seconds, their crisp texture almost melting. The result is a wonderful, light healthy soup that is both nourishing and comforting for the stomach. In many Chinese households soups are popular starters, so this recipe is ideal before a rich second course.

Preparation time: **5 minutes**        Cooking time: **8 minutes**

**1.** If you want to skin the tomatoes, cut a cross at the base of each one. Plunge them into a pan of boiling water for less than 1 minute then drain – the skin will peel off easily. Finely chop the flesh, discarding the hard centre.
**2.** Add the hot stock to the pan with the tomatoes. Pour the whisked egg into the broth, stirring gently. Add the soy, sesame oil, pepper and blended cornflour and mix well.
**3.** Shred in pieces of nori and add the spring onion. Serve immediately.

# Fried Prawn Dumplings (Xia Guo Tieh)
# with Soy Vinegar Dipping Sauce  makes 10

*300ml vegetable oil*

for the filling
*340g raw tiger prawns, shelled, deveined and*
*    finely chopped*
*2 tablespoons freshly grated ginger*
*4 garlic cloves, finely chopped*
*2 large spring onions, finely chopped*
*1 tablespoon shaosing rice wine or dry sherry*
*1 teaspoon sesame oil*
*1 tablespoon light soy sauce*
*pinch of salt and sugar*
*1 medium red chilli, deseeded and finely chopped*

*10 wonton wrappers*
*1 egg yolk*

for the soy vinegar dipping sauce
*2 tablespoons light soy sauce*
*2 tablespoons Chinese black rice vinegar*
*    or white wine vinegar*
*1 teaspoon finely chopped coriander leaves*
*    and stems*
*1 medium chilli, deseeded and finely chopped*

The trick to a good dumpling is to finely chop all the ingredients so that with each nibble the filling melts in the mouth with the detection of a little 'bite' between mouthfuls.

The tedious part is all the chopping and preparation but I promise you it pays: Xia Guo Tieh would be less delicious without the effort. The shortcut here is to use bought wonton flour wrappers from your local Chinese supermarket. They can be frozen so you can stock up. The dipping sauce is simple and the star ingredient – Chinese black rice vinegar – is aromatically earthy and delicately tangy.

Preparation time: **15 minutes**          Cooking time: **5 minutes**

**1.** Mix all the ingredients for the filling in a bowl. Stir well in a clockwise direction (we Chinese are very superstitious!).

**2.** Take a tablespoon of the filling and place in the centre of a wonton wrapper. Brush the edges of the wrapper with egg yolk and fold one corner to the other to form a triangular parcel. Press to seal then gather the sealed side of the parcel to form ripples around the edge of the dumpling. Repeat with the rest of the filling and wrappers.

**3.** Heat a wok or pan over high heat then add the oil (take care if frying in a wok). It is hot enough when a small piece of bread turns golden brown in 15 seconds. Fry the dumplings, in batches if necessary, and turn them so they do not overcook on one side. Fry until golden brown, for about 4–5 minutes. Once cooked, drain the excess oil from the dumplings on kitchen paper.

**4.** Mix all the ingredients for the soy vinegar dipping sauce and serve the dumplings immediately with the sauce.

# Vegetable Bao (Tzai Bao) makes 6

for the dough

1½ tablespoons sugar

125ml warm water

¾ teaspoon dried yeast (or 1½ teaspoons
    fresh yeast)

200g plain flour

1 tablespoon vegetable oil

¾ teaspoon baking powder

for the filling

1 tablespoon vegetable oil

2 garlic cloves, crushed and finely chopped

1 shallot, crushed and finely chopped

1 teaspoon freshly grated ginger root

small handful of gai lan (Chinese broccoli),
    leaves and stalks, washed and finely chopped

2 dried Chinese mushrooms, soaked in warm
    water for 20 minutes, stalks discarded,
    finely chopped

20g mock chicken (soya or gluten substitute)

handful of woodear mushrooms, soaked for
    20 minutes, finely chopped

1 handful tinned bamboo shoots, finely chopped

3 tablespoons light soy sauce

pinch of ground white pepper

dash of sesame oil

100g mung bean noodles, soaked and chopped

The Chinese festival of Ching-Ming is when people pay their respects to deceased relatives. On these auspicious days, it was customary to be vegetarian. I recall being taken by my grandmother on one occasion to visit the grave of my great-grandfather. I was daunted by the prospect. We paid our respects and burnt incense and said our prayers and I remember taking hold of my grandmother's hand because she looked so sad. She took me in her lap and we sat on a bench and tucked into her homemade Tzai Bao, which are these little buns. It was cold but comforting.

If you have the time, this recipe is very therapeutic and a joy to make. Great for a family occasion or as an afternoon tea treat.

Preparation time: **4 hours including proving**     Cooking time: **13 minutes**

1. To make the dough, dissolve the sugar in the water, add the yeast, stir gently, then leave for 8–10 minutes until frothy.

2. Sift the flour into a bowl, add the yeast mix and the oil and work into a dough. Lightly flour a work surface. Turn out and knead the dough until it is smooth and elastic (about 8 minutes). If it seems too sticky, knead in more flour.

3. Lightly oil a bowl, place the dough in it and lightly oil the surface of the dough. Cover with a damp tea towel and leave at room temperature to rise for 3 hours.

4. Once risen, uncover the dough, knock back, then turn onto a lightly floured surface. Flatten the dough, make a well in the centre and add the baking powder. Pinch all the sides together and lightly knead. Then roll into a long sausage about 3–4cm in diameter.

5. Cut the dough into 6 equal pieces. Form each piece into a ball, then roll out with a rolling pin and flatten to make discs about 10–12cm diameter and 0.5cm thick. Set aside on the floured surface and cover with clingfilm to prevent the dough from drying out.

6. Heat a wok over high heat then add the oil. Stir fry the filling ingredients in order, cooking each one for a few minutes before adding the next, and season with pepper and sesame oil. Throw in the drained mung bean noodles last and mix carefully so that they do not break up too much. Set aside the filling to cool.

7. Take the pieces of dough, place a large tablespoon of filling in the centre of each, pinch the sides of the dough to make the outer edges thinner than the centre then gather the sides to the middle, (when they are steamed the filling pushes through the top of the bun to spill open slightly.

8. Oil the base of a bamboo steamer and place the buns in the steamer. Fill a wok or pan with boiling water to a depth that will not immerse the base of the steamer and steam for about 7 minutes until the buns are opaque white. Test by inserting a toothpick into the centre of a bun – if it comes out clean and not doughy, as well as hot, you know it is ready.

# Stir-fried Fresh Beancurd, Pak Choy and Oyster Mushrooms in Black Bean Sauce serves 2

1 tablespoon vegetable oil
60g oyster mushrooms
200g pak choy leaves, separated
200g fresh tofu, cut into 2cm cubes
200ml hot vegetable stock
1 tablespoon cornflour blended with 2 tablespoons
    cold water (optional)

for the black bean sauce
1 tablespoon fermented, salted black beans
2 tablespoons light soy sauce
1 tablespoon shaosing rice wine or dry sherry
2 garlic cloves, crushed and finely chopped
1 red chilli, deseeded and finely chopped

fresh coriander sprigs

This is a favourite vegetarian recipe of mine, although if you are a meat lover you can add some minced beef after heating the vegetable oil in the method. There are many different varieties of beancurd (dofu to the Chinese, tofu to the Japanese – the name you see in supermarkets). It can be fresh, fried, fermented or smoked and is available in soft and firm varieties. The more acidic tofu is more silken in texture. Although in itself quite bland, when you fry or freeze a fresh block of tofu tiny holes appear, allowing it to soak up wonderful flavours like a sponge. Tofu is extremely nutritious and a good source of low-fat protein because it is made from the milky liquid of crushed soya beans which are pressed and formed to make this cheese-like ingredient.

Most ordinary supermarkets stock the long-life variety of tofu, packed in tetra-paks. However, nothing beats fresh beancurd and I would be thrilled to see fresh tofu next to the cheddar, mozzarella and stilton in the refrigerated section!

Preparation time: **10 minutes**          Cooking time: **5 minutes**

**1.** Blitz all the sauce ingredients in a food processor but do not process to a smooth sauce – you want to keep some texture to the sauce ingredients.
**2.** Heat a wok over high heat and add the oil. Throw in the mushrooms, pak choy and fresh tofu and stir fry for less than 1 minute.
**3.** Add the sauce and stir gently, taking care not to break up the delicate tofu.
**4.** Add the stock to the wok and bring to the boil. For a thicker sauce, add the blended cornflour and stir well.
**5.** Transfer to a large serving plate, garnish with fresh coriander and serve with steamed rice.

# Vegetarian-style Congee (Xi-fan) serves 4

2 tablespoons vegetable oil

2 garlic cloves, crushed and finely chopped

1 tablespoon freshly grated ginger

6 dried Chinese mushrooms, soaked in hot
    water for 20 minutes, stems discarded,
    finely chopped

1 small carrot, diced

200g brown basmati rice

200g healthy grain mix (green split peas,
    whole green lentils, whole grain, barley flakes,
    pearl barley)

3 litres boiling water

1 red pepper, finely diced

1 litre vegetable stock

handful of tinned bamboo shoots, chopped

2 tablespoons light soy sauce

1 tablespoon toasted sesame oil

pinch of freshly ground black pepper

small handful of coriander leaves and stems,
    chopped

Xi-fan, meaning 'watery rice', is a simple concoction of rice cooked in a lot of water, otherwise known as congee. You can have an array of ingredients from seafood to a vegetarian mix. As a child, whenever I stayed with my grandparents, we would have a big bowl of Xi-fan (the plain variety) for breakfast accompanied with small dishes of pickled cucumber, spicy pickled bamboo shoots, salted peanuts, fried eggs, and fermented dofu (tofu). My grandparents ate very simply and being farmers were always up at the crack of dawn (something my brother and I were never used to). When I feel nostalgic I make myself such a breakfast. My modern vegetarian-style Xi-fan with brown rice and mixed whole grains also does the job and gives me a comforting fix whenever I need one.

Preparation time: **8 minutes**       Cooking time: **40 minutes**

**1.** Heat a wok over high heat and add the oil.
**2.** Stir fry the garlic and ginger and Chinese mushrooms for less than 1 minute. Add the carrot, brown rice and whole grain mix. Stir fry for less than 1 minute and add 1 litre boiling water. Let the rice cook for 25–30 minutes, stirring and adding up to a further 2 litres water to make sure the rice and grains are thoroughly cooked. Add the red pepper, stir well then pour in the vegetable stock. Finally add the bamboo shoots and season with the light soy sauce, sesame oil and ground black pepper.
**3.** Sprinkle in the chopped coriander and serve immediately.

# Steamed Fiery Beancurd

serves 2

*400g fresh tofu*
*2 tablespoons vegetable oil*
*3 tablespoons light soy sauce*
*1 tablespoon sesame oil*
*1 spring onion, sliced lengthways*
*1 red chilli, deseeded and finely chopped*
*small bunch of coriander, chopped*

A simple and mouthwatering dish ready in minutes. If you are not a big fan of beancurd (dofu or tofu) you can substitute fish or vegetables as the sauce complements most proteins, and it's really healthy too!

**Preparation time: 5 minutes**        **Cooking time: 5 minutes**

**1.** Place the block of tofu on a heatproof plate. Cut into 2cm squares, but keep it as a block. Place the heatproof plate inside a bamboo steamer. Fill a wok or pan with boiling water to a depth that will not submerge the base of the steamer. Place the steamer in the wok and steam for 2 minutes.

**2.** Heat a wok over high heat and add the vegetable oil. Add the soy sauce and sesame oil and give it a good stir. Add the spring onion and chilli and and stir for less than 20 seconds. Add the coriander then quickly take the wok off the heat.

**3.** Remove the tofu from the steamer and drain any excess liquid from the plate.

**4.** Pour the fiery soy sauce over the tofu and serve immediately with steamed rice.

# Pan-fried Prawns and Sweet Chilli Jam   serves 2

12 (about 170g shelled weight) whole raw
    tiger prawns, shelled but tail on, deveined
    and washed
3–5 tablespoons olive oil
pinch of sea salt and ground white pepper

for the batter
1 egg, beaten
50g potato flour

fresh coriander leaves

to serve
Sweet Chilli Jam (see page 142)
jasmine green tea

Seasoned tiger prawns, dipped in egg batter then lightly fried and served with sweet and fiery chilli jam. Yum. Eat this dish in true Chinese style with a selection of home-cooked dishes washed down with copious amounts of Chinese green tea. In fact, Chinese green tea gives this dish balance and makes it a lot healthier. Where's the rationale? My late grandfather used to swear by Chinese green tea. He was a slim cheerful man who loved singing karaoke at the local Old Gentleman's Club in the village of Chiao Tao where my father grew up. When I was eight, he said: 'Ching-He, always remember this, drink plenty of Chinese green tea and you will never get fat. Look at me. I eat so much and see how slim I am?' Oh grandfather, you were always wise and full of eccentricity.

Preparation: **5 minutes**        Cooking time: **12 minutes**

**1.** First make the chilli jam (see page 142).
**2.** Place the prawns in a bowl and season with salt and pepper.
**3.** Combine the egg and potato flour in a bowl to make a batter. Mix the batter with the prawns and coat well.
**4.** Heat a wok or pan over high heat, and add the olive oil. Fry the prawns by throwing them in one at a time. When they turn pink and the coating turns golden brown, remove and drain of any excess oil on kitchen paper.
**5.** Garnish with some coriander and serve with the chilli jam and steamed rice… don't forget the jasmine green tea.

# Ginger, Chilli and Soy Steamed Scallops

**serves 2 as a selection of mains**

10 scallops on the shell

for the sauce
1 garlic clove, finely chopped
1 teaspoon freshly grated ginger
1 medium red chilli, deseeded and finely chopped
3 teaspoons light soy sauce
1 teaspoon sesame oil
2 teaspoons finely chopped coriander leaves
    and stems

150ml vegetable oil
12 garlic cloves, chopped into small pieces
50g shallots, chopped into small pieces
small handful of coriander leaves, shredded

This is a traditional Chinese recipe and fresh scallops are a must. If you don't know how to clean the scallops, get your local fishmonger to prepare them for you, but do ask for the shells as these not only present the scallops beautifully, they also retain the scallops' flavours and sweet juices once steamed. The way to eat these is to pop a scallop in your mouth then bring your lips to the shell and drink the delicious juices. Ideally this dish is presented and served with other meat and vegetable dishes at the table and shared and accompanied with jasmine rice. However, they can also make for a delicious starter for two.

Preparation time: **10 minutes**          Cooking time: **6 minutes**

1. Prise open the scallop shells if necessary using a sharp chopping knife. Cut through the muscle that attaches the scallop to its shell and wash the scallops and shells well under cold running water. Discard the corals if you prefer. Place each scallop back on one shell and place these in 2 large bamboo steamers.
2. Combine all the sauce ingredients in a bowl and spoon 1 teaspoon of the dressing over the scallops.
3. Stack one bamboo steamer on top of the other and place the lid on the top.
4. Pour 1.5 litres water into a wide-based wok and bring to the boil. Place the bamboo steamers in the wok making sure the base is not immersed and steam for 5–6 minutes.
5. Meanwhile, heat a small pan and add the vegetable oil. Deep fry the garlic and shallots until crispy, then strain the oil and collect the crispy garnish and drain on kitchen paper.
6. When the scallops are cooked they will be opaque white and slightly firm to the touch. Remove them from the steamer, garnish with shredded coriander and sprinkle with the crispy garlic and shallots. Serve immediately.

# Steamed Sea Bass in Stir-fried Yellow Bean Sauce serves 2

2 whole sea bass, head off if preferred, descaled
    and cleaned
2 tablespoons shaosing rice wine or dry sherry
4 tablespoons groundnut oil
4 garlic cloves, crushed and finely chopped
2 tablespoons freshly grated ginger
4 tablespoons yellow bean sauce
8 tablespoons light soy sauce
2 tablespoons toasted sesame oil
1 large spring onion, chopped
small handful of coriander leaves, chopped
pinch of salt and freshly ground black pepper

This is the perfect recipe to serve at Chinese New Year as the Mandarin word for fish is 'Yu', which also sounds like the 'Yu' in the Chinese phrase 'Nian Nian You Yu', which means 'Every year you have abundance' whether it's wealth, health, happiness, luck or love. This is a phrase you say to family and friends to wish them well in the New Year. The Chinese are superstitious and believe that you should serve the fish whole including the head as it symbolises completeness and unity. So if it is Chinese New Year and you are serving this recipe, please ask your fishmonger to keep the head on! The Chinese New Year falls on a different day each year and follows the lunar calendar. There are many customs and one of them is to give Hong-Bao meaning 'red packets', red envelopes stuffed with money to give to your elders or young children... as a child I must admit I thought this was the best bit! The colour red is also very symbolic and is a very lucky colour so on this occasion perhaps sea bass would not be the ultimate choice and instead you might choose a red mullet.

Preparation time: **5 minutes**　　　Cooking time: **7 minutes**

**1.** Wash the fish in cold water. Pat the fish dry with kitchen paper. Cut some slits into the skin of the fish. Season with salt and pepper and place them on a heatproof plate and transfer to a bamboo steamer. Pour the shaosing rice wine over the fish.

**2.** Fill a wok or pan with boiling water to a depth that will not immerse the base of the steamer. Place the lid on the steamer and steam for 12 minutes.

**3.** Heat another small pan or wok over high heat and add the groundnut oil.

**4.** Stir fry the garlic and ginger for less than 1 minute. Add the yellow bean sauce and light soy sauce and stir well. Add a few dashes of toasted sesame oil.

**5.** Add the spring onions and coriander to the wok and take it quickly off the heat.

**6.** Pour the sauce over the steamed fish and serve immediately with Jasmine Rice and Steamed Pak Choy (see pages 142 and 146).

# Steamed Cod with Salted Black Beans   serves 2

500g cod fillet, skinned or unskinned
2 garlic cloves, crushed and finely chopped
2 tablespoons ginger, grated
3 tablespoons sesame oil
3 tablespoons light soy sauce
2 tablespoons rice wine
juice of 1 lime
2 tablespoons bought dried fermented, salted
    black beans, rinsed and crushed
1 spring onion, chopped diagonally into
    1cm pieces
sea salt and freshly ground black pepper

This is a family recipe served time and time again at home. I find it a godsend after a busy day at work. Not only is it unfussy to cook, it is healthy and nutritious too. Great to serve at a dinner party and presenting it in the bamboo steamers gives it authentic Chinese flair. This is a truly fast dish, provided of course you have the fish, fresh limes and spring onions in your fridge – the rest are store cupboard ingredients. You can also use any other firm white fish, such as halibut or sea bass in this recipe. Delicious accompaniments are jasmine rice and Chinese pickled salad.

Preparation time: **5 minutes**          Cooking time: **12 minutes**

**1.** Wash the fish in cold running water, pat dry on kitchen paper, then slash some slits into the skin of the fish (if necessary). Season with a pinch of salt and ground black pepper on both sides.

**2.** If the skin is on, place the fish on a heatproof plate, skin side down. Put the rest of the ingredients except the spring onion over the fish and place the plate in the base of a bamboo steamer. Fill a wok or pan with boiling water to a depth that will not submerge the base of the steamer. Place the steamer in the wok, put the lid on and steam for 12 minutes on a high heat. One minute before the fish is ready, add the spring onions and season to taste.

**3.** Serve immediately with Jasmine Rice and some of my Chinese Pickled Salad (see pages 142 and 146).

# Peking-style Duck with Savoury–Sour Mushroom and Ginger Sauce on Udon Noodles serves 2

2 duck breast fillets, skin on, scored criss-cross
    fashion
120g dried udon noodles

for the Peking duck marinade
$^1/_2$ teaspoon Chinese five-spice powder
1 tablespoon sesame oil
3 tablespoons hoi sin sauce
3 tablespoons brown sugar
3 tablespoons clear honey
1 tablespoon dark soy sauce

for the mushroom and ginger sauce
1 tablespoon groundnut oil
1 garlic clove, crushed and finely chopped
1 tablespoon freshly grated ginger
400ml chicken stock
2 dried Chinese mushrooms, soaked in hot
    water for 20 minutes, stems discarded, chopped
small handful of shredded Chinese Leaf
small handful of beansprouts
1 tablespoon light soy sauce
1 tablespoon shaosing rice wine or dry sherry
1 tablespoon rice vinegar
1 tablespoon cornflour blended with 2
    tablespoons cold water
1 spring onion, finely chopped
salt and ground white pepper

small handful of coriander leaves, finely chopped

I sometimes cook this dish at home and I think it's equally impressive to serve for dinner guests too. The succulent duck complements the savoury–sour sauce well and, combined with the texture of the noodles, makes this a wonderful dish. In true Chinese spirit and style, it is customary to slurp the noodles and soup together, adding air to the soup and allowing your taste buds full access to all the flavours... though perhaps an experience you can try without your dinner guests? My dear parents sometimes forget while out for the evening and this always has their guests in little fits of giggles.

Preparation time: **10 minutes plus marinating**      Cooking time: **45 minutes**

1. First make the Peking duck marinade. Mix all the ingredients in a bowl, pour into a zip lock bag, add the duck and marinate for as long as possible, ideally overnight.
2. Preheat the oven to 180°C/350°F/Gas Mark 4.
3. Remove the duck breast from the marinade and place in a hot pan (no oil), skin side down, and cook for approximately 1 minute on each side until golden brown. Then transfer to the oven and cook for 20–30 minutes, depending on the size of the duck breast and how well done you like it (20 minutes will be slightly pink in the middle).
4. Meanwhile, cook the noodles according to the instructions on the packet, drain then refresh under cold running water and set aside.
5. To make the sauce, heat a pan over high heat, add the groundnut oil and stir fry the garlic and ginger for less than 1 minute. Add the chicken stock and throw in the vegetables. Season with light soy sauce, rice wine, rice vinegar and salt and pepper. Bring the sauce to the boil, add the blended cornflour and stir well. Reduce the heat.
6. Remove the duck from the oven and let it rest for 1 minute.
7. Sprinkle the spring onion into the sauce.
8. Refresh the noodles with boiling water from the kettle, drain, then make a bed of noodles in a deep serving plate and ladle over some of the mushroom and ginger sauce. Slice the duck and arrange on top of the vegetables, sprinkle some chopped coriander over the top and serve immediately.

# Zhejiang Mein  *serves 2*

for the sauce
*250ml chicken stock*
*3 tablespoons hoi sin sauce*
*2 tablespoons shaosing rice wine or dry sherry*
*1 tablespoon chilli bean sauce*

*1 tablespoon groundnut oil*
*2 garlic cloves, crushed and finely chopped*
*350g minced beef*
*200g dried vermicelli rice noodles*

to garnish
*1 spring onion, finely chopped*
*small handful of coriander leaves, finely chopped*
*1 small carrot, finely sliced into matchsticks*

Zhejiang Mein means 'mixed well sauce noodle' in Mandarin Chinese. It may not sound inspiring but it certainly inspired my friends when they tried it! This is a well-known Taiwanese noodle dish and again I am truly grateful to my mother for remembering this one among so many delightful recipes. You would never have a dish like this in a Chinese restaurant, which is why this dish is so special. It's really simple: the trick is to let the sauce reduce to a few spoonfuls as all the flavours are soaked up into the meat. Try to buy minced beef with an even amount of fat and meat unless you are watching the calories. When my mother is in a vegetarian mood she substitutes the beef with unflavoured soya protein mince which you can get in supermarkets or health stores... just as tasty!

Preparation time: **5 minutes**          Cooking time: **10 minutes**

**1.** Combine the sauce ingredients in a bowl.
**2.** Heat a wok over high heat and add the oil. Stir fry the garlic for less than 1 minute. Add the beef to the wok and stir fry for about 1 minute until browned.
**3.** Pour in the sauce, bring to the boil and cook for about 4 minutes to allow the sauce to reduce. Transfer the sauce to a plate or bowl, cover with foil and keep warm.
**4.** Cook the noodles according to the instructions on the packet, drain then divide between 2 bowls. Spoon over the meat sauce and sprinkle with spring onions, coriander and carrot strips and serve immediately.

# Bamboo-wrapped Chicken and Glutinous Rice (Zong-zi) makes 6

for the chicken

*1 tablespoon groundnut oil*

*1 large skinless chicken breast, cut into*
*even-sized chunks*

*3 tablespoons light soy sauce*

*1 tablespoon dark soy sauce*

*1 teaspoon Chinese five-spice powder*

*pinch of ground white pepper*

*3 tablespoons groundnut oil*

*1 tablespoon freshly grated ginger*

*4 garlic cloves, crushed and finely chopped*

*4 medium shallots, peeled and finely chopped*

*5 dried Chinese mushrooms, soaked in hot water*
*for 20 minutes, stalks discarded, finely chopped*

*40g dried baby shrimp, soaked in hot water for*
*20 minutes*

*50g toasted cashew nuts*

*600g cooked glutinous rice (300g washed*
*glutinous rice cooked in 500ml water)*

*4 tablespoons light soy sauce*

*1 tablespoon sesame oil*

*2 pinches of Chinese five-spice powder*

*12 bamboo leaves (or lotus leaves), soaked in*
*cold water then blanched in boiling water*

*6 x 30cm lengths of string*

Zong-zi is traditionally eaten on Duan Wu Jie, the Dragon Boat Festival to mark the fifth day of the fifth lunar calendar in 277 BC. The poet Chu Yuan was loved and greatly respected by the people of China. Many mourned his death by throwing cooked rice wrapped in bamboo leaves (known as zong-zi), into the river so that the fish would not feed on his corpse. On this memorable occasion, dragon boat races are held and zong-zi is eaten. Traditionally there are both sweet and savoury fillings. A sweet one would be red bean paste; savoury would be egg yolk with braised soy belly pork. This modern adaptation was given to me by my grandmother and it is our family version of savoury zong-zi. They make great meals or snacks served with soy sauce or sweet chilli jam. They can also be frozen and reheated for when you get a craving. Enjoy!

Preparation time: **10 minutes**          Cooking time: **40 minutes**

1. For the chicken, heat a wok over high heat and add the oil. Mix the chicken pieces with the rest of the ingredients then tip into the wok and stir fry for about 2–3 minutes on high heat until browned and cooked. Remove and set aside.

2. Wipe out the wok with kitchen paper, reheat and add the oil. Throw in the ginger, garlic, shallots and soaked mushrooms and stir fry for less than 1 minute. Add the dried shrimp and cashew nuts and stir fry for less than 1 minute. Add the cooked rice and mix all the ingredients well. Season with light soy sauce, sesame oil and five-spice powder and give a final stir. Remove from the heat and set aside.

3. Select two bamboo leaves, one small and one large. Place the smaller leaf on the larger one with the pointed end of the leaves at opposite ends. Fold the leaves in half, cup them in your hand and fold one edge of the leaves down so that they form a conical shape in your palm. With the leaves pointing towards you, wet your other hand and scoop some of the rice mixture into the cup. Top with 2–3 chicken pieces, then add more rice mix to fill. Wrap the other end of the leaves around the opening to form a closed pyramid. Take a piece of string, loop it around the triangular corner of the wrapped rice and wrap around the bamboo parcel twice, tying it to secure. Repeat to make 6 parcels.

4. The zong-zi are then ready to eat. To reheat and ensure real flavour, place the parcels in a bamboo steamer. Fill a wok or pan with boiling water to a depth that will not immerse the base of the steamer and steam for 2–3 minutes. Alternatively, place in a pan of boiling water for 4 minutes. Serve with soy sauce or Sweet Chilli Jam (see page 142).

# Taiwanese-style Pepper Steak and Egg on Steamed Rice serves 2

2 x 250g sirloin steaks

for the marinade
5 tablespoons light soy sauce
2 tablespoons Chinese five-spice powder
1 tablespoon brown sugar
2 tablespoons ground black pepper

3 tablespoons groundnut oil
2 eggs

Jasmine Rice (see page 142)

Some might say this peppery dish is rather like a Western-style steak. It is similar but instead of finding it in steak houses, it can be bought on street stands in Taiwan. Most night markets in Taipei City, such as the bustling Shilin night market or Huashi Street, still sell street food with delicacies to be sampled and savoured. The flavours that waft down the streets make your mouth water even on a full stomach! Whenever I visited Taiwan on my summer holidays, my cousins would take me on their mopeds and we would whizz to the markets to have this dish and many others, from Tso Do-fu ('stinky tofu') to Eara-Tzen ('oyster omelettes'). The Chinese five-spice makes you crave this recipe again and again.

Preparation time: **10 minutes plus marinating**
Cooking time: **30 minutes with the rice**

1. Combine all the marinade ingredients in a bowl and place the steak in the marinade for 30 minutes (overnight is better, but even 10 minutes is fine).
2. Heat a wok over high heat and add 2 tablespoons groundnut oil. Remove the steak from the marinade and fry the steak for 1 minute on one side then turn it over, to brown the other side. Pour in the rest of the marinade and cook until the meat is done according to your preference. I like it medium so about 6 minutes, depending on the size of the steak.
3. A few minutes before the steak is ready, heat another small pan add the remaining oil, and fry the eggs. Cook to your preference but the yolks are supposed to be quite runny.
4. To serve, place some jasmine rice in a small bowl, then invert it onto a plate in an attractive mound. Place the steak in the middle, place the egg on top of the steak and pour the steak cooking juices over the egg, meat and rice.

# Five-spice Saucy Chicken Stir Fry    serves 2

350g skinless chicken breast, sliced then cut into
    even-sized chunks
2 tablespoons oyster sauce
1¹/₂ tablespoons cornflour
pinch of salt and ground white pepper

1 tablespoon groundnut oil
2 garlic cloves, crushed and finely chopped
1 tablespoon freshly grated ginger
1 teaspoon crushed dried red chillies
250ml fresh chicken stock
1 small carrot, sliced lengthways into strips
200g pak choy, washed, leaves separated
    but left whole
2 tablespoons dark soy sauce
2 tablespoons shaosing rice wine or dry sherry
¹/₂ teaspoon Chinese five-spice powder
1 tablespoon cornflour blended with 2 tablespoons
    cold water
1 spring onion, finely chopped

I love saucy stir fries but don't get me wrong, a dry stir fry is great too. It is, though, really comforting to have a steaming saucy stir-fry dish with plain steamed rice, especially on a cold day. This dish works well because it's not very heavy and all the ingredients fuse well in the dish allowing you to savour hints of the hot and spicy garlic, ginger, star anise (from the five spice), pepper, soy and the sweetness of the honey. The vegetables at the end add delightful crunch and texture. The chicken is also very 'happening' – it is first marinated then covered in cornflour which gives it a bouncy texture once cooked. How can a dish so simple taste so irresistible?

Preparation time: **10 minutes**      Cooking time: **10 minutes**

**1.** Place the chicken in a bowl and season with oyster sauce, salt, ground white pepper and cornflour. Set aside.

**2.** Heat a wok over high heat and add the groundnut oil. Throw in the garlic and ginger and stir fry for less than 1 minute. Add the chicken breast and stir fry for about 3–4 minutes until golden brown. Season with the crushed dried chillies.

**3.** Add the chicken stock, carrot, pak choy and season with dark soy, shaosing rice wine, and five-spice powder and bring to the boil. Add the blended cornflour and stir well.

**4.** Sprinkle over the spring onions and serve with Jasmine Rice (see page 142).

# Pan-fried Pork Noodle Soup  serves 1

1 pork chop or loin steak
2 tablespoons hoi sin sauce
80g dried yellow shi noodles (or other variety)

for the soup
500ml chicken stock
3 dried Chinese mushrooms, soaked in hot water
    for 20 minutes, whole
80g Chinese leaf, shredded
3 tablespoons light soy sauce
3 tablespoons shaosing rice wine or dry sherry
2 tablespoons rice vinegar
40g beansprouts
50g spring onions, chopped lengthways
pinch of salt and freshly ground black pepper

fresh coriander leaves

A quick and easy dinner that is nutritious and healthy. What will speed up the cooking of this dish is to have some Chinese mushrooms presoaked. I always have a small measuring jug of water with some Chinese mushrooms soaking, ready to pick out and use. I would do this the night before and replenish every evening. However, if you don't have this habit then you can soak them in hot water, 20 minutes before cooking, which speeds up the softening process. Another shortcut is to buy straight to wok noodles. All the same, I prefer to cook mine from dried in boiling water, that way I can cook them really al dente the way I like them, just like cooking pasta. There are many dried varieties to try: green tea noodles, buckwheat, wholewheat, flat udon and more... you can have a different variation every time!

Preparation time: **20 minutes plus marinating**          Cooking time: **10 minutes**

**1.** Marinate the pork in the hoi sin sauce for as long as possible (overnight is best).
**2.** Preheat a griddle pan and cook the marinated pork for about 5 minutes until golden brown on each side.
**3.** Meanwhile cook the noodles according to the instructions on the packet, refresh under cold water then drain and set aside.
**4.** Bring the chicken stock to a simmer in a wok or pan and add the mushrooms. Throw in the shredded Chinese leaf and season with light soy sauce, rice wine and rice vinegar.
**5.** Remove the pork from the griddle pan and set aside to rest.
**6.** Add the cooked noodles to the wok along with the beansprouts. Season further to taste then sprinkle in the spring onions.
**7.** To serve, ladle some of the noodle soup into a bowl, slice the pork and place on the noodles and garnish with fresh coriander.

# Salty Crispy Chicken (Sien Shu Gi) serves 2

250g skinless chicken thighs, each thigh piece
   chopped in half across the bone
50g potato flour
5 tablespoons groundnut oil

for the marinade
2 garlic cloves, minced
1 tablespoon light soy sauce
$^1/_2$ tablespoon salt
$^1/_2$ tablespoon Chinese five-spice powder
1 teaspoon sesame oil

1 medium red chilli, deseeded and finely chopped
$^1/_2$ spring onion, green parts only, finely chopped

Sien Shu Gi is to die for: simple yet scrumptious. It's a famous street snack in Taiwan. On a recent visit I stole (or rather hovered) around the street-hawker stand, watching the chef prepare this, determined not to leave the country without it. In the end I bribed him. (Just kidding!) Here is my adapted version, with chicken thighs as the meat is a lot juicier than breast. Drumsticks work well too. Good accompaniments would be steamed rice or chunky chips and a cold beer.

Preparation time: **5 minutes plus marinating**      Cooking time: **7 minutes**

**1.** Mix all the marinade ingredients in a bowl and add the chicken pieces, turning to coat. For best results leave in the fridge overnight.
**2.** Coat the chicken pieces in potato flour.
**3.** Heat a wok or pan and add the oil. Add the chicken and fry lightly for 5–6 minutes until the thighs are golden brown on all sides. Drain the chicken of any excess oil on kitchen paper.
**4.** Serve sprinkled with finely chopped chilli and spring onion and a portion of chunky chips.

# Taiwanese-style Nuoromein  serves 2

1 tablespoon groundnut oil
2 garlic cloves, crushed and finely chopped
1 tablespoon freshly grated ginger
1 red chilli, deseeded and chopped
1 large shallot, finely chopped
½ onion, chopped
1 small carrot, chopped
200g stewing beef
400ml vegetable or beef stock
1 tablespoon chilli bean sauce
1 teaspoon chilli sauce
1 teaspoon dark soy sauce
2 teaspoons brown sugar
2 tablespoons cornflour blended with
    2 tablespoons water
180g dried flat udon noodles

to garnish
1 spring onion, finely chopped
handful of chopped coriander leaves

Nuoromein, meaning 'beef-style noodle', is Taiwan's favourite snack and you can find it on most street-hawker stands throughout the island. Ask anyone on the street and they all have an opinion about this dish. Everyone is very passionate about what ingredients go into it and how they like it with extra chillies, so there are a few variations. The dish is based on the style of cooking from Sichuan province in China and it fuses plenty of chillies, garlic and ginger to make a fiery snack. Of course, you can adjust the amount of chillies to your liking but you would be missing out on *la pièce de résistance*!

Preparation time: **5 minutes**          Cooking time: **40 minutes**

**1.** Put all the ingredients down to the cornflour into a large pot and cook over medium heat for 40 minutes. The longer you cook the stew the more mouthwatering the dish is as the beef softens and takes on the flavour of the sauce. At the end of the cooking process, stir in the blended cornflour to thicken the sauce. Cover and set aside.

**2.** Cook the noodles according to the instructions on the packet, drain then refresh under cold running water and set aside. Just before serving refresh the noodles with boiling water from the kettle, drain, and divide between 2 bowls. Ladle some delicious stew over the noodles, sprinkle with freshly chopped spring onion and coriander and serve immediately.

# Braised Belly Pork and Aubergine in Chilli Bean Sauce serves 4

2 tablespoons groundnut oil

2 garlic cloves, chopped

1 tablespoon freshly grated ginger

4 large chillies, deseeded and chopped

4 dried Chinese mushrooms, soaked in hot
    water for 20 minutes, stalks discarded, sliced

450g belly pork, chopped into rectangular
    pieces 1.5cm thick

1 large aubergine, cut into 1cm cubes

500ml vegetable stock

2 tablespoons chilli bean sauce

2 tablespoons dark soy sauce

1 tablespoon light soy sauce

pinch of salt and freshly ground black pepper

to garnish

4 large spring onions, sliced lengthways

small handful of chopped coriander leaves

This dish is a chilli winter warmer – the belly pork is fatty yet satisfying and soaks up the delicious juices of the fiery stew, while the aubergine absorbs all the flavours like a sponge. When you're short on time, cook this in a wok, like a stir fry, which is what I usually do – just follow the method below. However, if you have a free lazy Sunday afternoon, try cooking this dish as a casserole for 45 minutes, adding the aubergine about 20 minutes after the start of cooking and the spring onions at the last minute. The slow-cooking method breaks down the pork making it really tender. Either way, it tastes great. For a vegetarian version, follow the recipe and add some Chinese leaf or greens and cubes of dofu (tofu or beancurd) instead of the pork. Add the dofu after the aubergines and stir gently as it breaks up easily.

Preparation: **10 minutes**          Cooking time: **12 minutes**

**1.** Heat a wok or pan over high heat and add the oil. Throw in the garlic, ginger, chillies and Chinese mushrooms and stir fry for less than 1 minute. Add the belly pork and stir fry for another 2 minutes until browned. Throw in the aubergines and stir fry for a further 2 minutes.

**2.** Pour in 500ml vegetable stock and stir well. Add the chilli bean sauce, dark soy sauce and light soy sauce. Season to taste and cook until the meat is tender and the aubergines have softened.

**3.** Garnish with spring onions and coriander and serve with steamed rice.

# Chinese Egg Custard Tarts (Dan-ta) makes 12

200g ready-made sweet pastry
butter for greasing

for the filling
2 small eggs at room temperature, lightly beaten
75g caster sugar
375ml evaporated milk

Crumbly pastry with a yummy not-so-sweet set egg custard in the middle. Once again, I have my mother to thank for this lovely recipe. An egg tart was sometimes my after-school treat – delicious straight out of the oven, washed down with a glass of cold soya milk. You often find these little delights in dim sum restaurants too and they can be made with puff pastry (equally tasty). Dan-ta resemble the Portuguese tarts (*pasteis de nata*) and it may have been Portuguese travellers who introduced this recipe to the Orient, for they sailed the South China Seas and landed in Taiwan – my birth country – in the 16th century, calling it Ilha Formosa, meaning 'beautiful island'.

Preparation time: **15 minutes**      Cooking time: **25 minutes**

**1.** Preheat the oven to 200°C/400°F/Gas Mark 6 and lightly grease a 12-hole tart pan with some butter.
**2.** Roll out the pastry on a board to about 3mm thick. Cut out 12 circles using a 7cm round cutter and line the tart holes with the pastry circles.
**3.** Put the filling ingredients in a small bowl and beat lightly until smooth. Pour the filling into the pastry-lined tart pans but leaving 6mm at the top.
**4.** Bake the tarts for about 10 minutes, then reduce the heat to 180°C/350°F/Gas Mark 4. Bake for a further 10–15 minutes until the custard has set. Test by inserting a small toothpick – it should come out clean. These can be served cold, but are much nicer warm!

# Banana, Raisin and Chocolate Fried Wontons  serves 2/makes 8

3 ripe bananas, sliced 1cm thick
8 pieces of milk chocolate
24 raisins
8 wonton wrappers

vegetable oil for deep frying

Not a very healthy dessert but then again desserts rarely are, especially the tasty ones and this is one of those. Here, wonton wrappers (available ready-made in Chinese supermarkets) provide the wrap for fresh bananas, chocolates and raisins and are bundled together, deep-fried and served with vanilla ice cream. This is not a very traditional recipe but a sexy way of using wonton wrappers, which my mother taught me. You can also ring the changes and make a few with fresh lychees instead of bananas, as that combination with melted chocolate is just as heavenly.

Preparation time: **5 minutes**    Cooking time: **7 minutes**

1. Place 2 slices of banana, 3 raisins and a piece of milk chocolate in the centre of each wonton wrapper.
2. Dip your finger in a small bowl of water and wet the four sides of the wonton wrapper.
3. Bring the four edges to the centre, hold down and twist so that they look like wontons.
4. Heat a wok over high heat, add vegetable oil to a little less than half full and heat to 180°/350°F or until a piece of bread browns in 15 seconds. Deep fry the wontons until golden brown, remove with a slotted spoon and drain on kitchen paper.
5. Serve immediately – they're very good with vanilla ice cream.

# Taro and Sago Sweet Soup    serves 4

*300g taro, peeled*
*60g sago, soaked in cold water for 30 minutes*
*1 litre boiling water*
*55g rock sugar*
*500ml water*
*125ml coconut milk*
*230ml fresh milk*

Taro is a popular root vegetable used not only in China but throughout the Orient. It is also known as cocoyam and the 'potato of the Far East'. There are many varieties. They have a brownish skin and the flesh may be purple, beige or white. The variety I always go for in this recipe is purple fleshed to give this sweet dessert soup a gorgeous purple colour, but it is more likely to be the white-fleshed variety you find in Chinese supermarkets. Taro needs to be boiled for a long time to ensure it is really tender but a good trick is to steam it. Sago is a powdery starch obtained from the sago palm. It is made into granules which, when heated, become sticky little pearls that make a delicious accompaniment in this sweet coconut-based dessert. It is equally good hot or cold.

Preparation time: **30 minutes**    Cooking time: **35 minutes**

**1.** Cut 100g of the peeled taro into 1.5cm cubes and place on a heatproof plate in a steamer. Fill a wok or pan with boiling water to a depth that will not immerse the base of the steamer. Place the steamer in the wok and steam for 15 minutes.

**2.** Meanwhile, purée the remaining 200g taro in a blender.

**3.** Drain the sago and place in a pan with 1 litre boiling water and simmer for 10 minutes, then turn off the heat and leave for 10 minutes until the sago turns transparent. Rinse it in boiled water and drain well.

**4.** Put the rock sugar with the 500ml water in a pan and simmer until dissolved. Add the taro purée, stir well and bring to the boil. Add the sago to the pan and stir well. Pour in the coconut milk, fresh milk and add the already steamed taro cubes, bring to the boil again and serve immediately.

# Crêpes with Red Bean Paste

# and Vanilla Ice Cream   makes 8 small or 4 large crêpes

150g plain flour
pinch of salt
1 egg, beaten
300ml milk
4–8 tablespoons vegetable oil
200g red bean paste
500ml vanilla ice cream
100ml maple syrup

Red beans, otherwise known as adzuki or azuki, are usually used in desserts in China because of their nutty sweet flavour. They are boiled, then sugar is added and blended into a paste which is used as a filling in moon cakes (eaten during the Autumn Moon Festival every year) and sweet rice flour dumplings. The Chinese believe they have a 'yang' (heat-giving) nature and help balance out a diet that is too 'yin' (cooling). These beans are really nutritious with 25 per cent protein. When I was growing up, my mother would make a red bean soup, which she always believed helped to cleanse the kidneys. This is my red bean paste dessert, not a traditional dish but I thought I would make a modern recipe with such a traditional Chinese ingredient. You can buy ready-made, sweetened adzuki red bean paste in tins in Chinese supermarkets or you can make your own. However, ready-made helps to reduce the preparation time, and why not?

Preparation time: **5 minutes**          Cooking time: **15 minutes**

**1.** Sift the flour and salt in a bowl. Add the egg and milk and stir to make a smooth batter.

**2.** Preheat the oven to 150°C/300°C/Gas Mark 2.

**3.** Heat 1 tablespoon oil in a frying pan and ladle in enough batter to make 1 large or 1 small crêpe. When small holes appear, flip over and cook the other side.

**4.** Place on a plate, cover, and keep warm in the oven while you make the rest.

**5.** Heat the red bean paste in a small pan until warmed.

**6.** Spread a layer of the red bean paste onto each crêpe and fold. Top with a scoop of vanilla ice cream, drizzle over some maple syrup and serve immediately.

# 3. West Meets East

From Chicken and Shiitake Mushroom Pie, Guandong Duck with Mango Salsa to Chinese-style Seafood Risotto and Lychee and Mango Trifle – this is fusion Chinese pushed to the limit!

From my varied background and childhood experiences of living in different countries (indeed, continents), I have learnt that mixing and matching is what food is about. If there were no particular ingredients in my store cupboard or fridge, I would often improvise rather than walk to my local shop – not because I was lazy, but because it was a challenge and I was quite an adventurous child. When I have a craving for a classic dish, I will always try to make it different every time, by adding a new ingredient or varying the cooking technique. Discovering and inventing are part of the pleasure of being a cook.

There were no fixed rules when the recipes for this chapter were born. The ingredients are as wide ranging as arborio rice, parsnips and banana leaves. There are some classics, such as fish and chips but made with a Chinese twist, and my Taiwanese-style Chicken Caesar Salad where the chicken has been prepared in a way that city professionals of Taiwan would recognise as similar to the fried pork cutlet (Za Pai Gu) which is a popular choice for their packed lunch. There are endless possibilities of fusion Chinese if we only let ourselves think outside of the box. Of course, the basics can be learnt from family, friends and recipe books but sometimes the most delicious dishes are created when you add that special touch or you go one step further. I hope I have given you a few ideas to get you on your own path towards experimenting and creating delectable original dishes at home to suit any occasion.

# Chinese Chorizo, Roast Sweet Pepper and Cherry Tomato Melt

serves 4/makes 20

5 Lap-Cheong sausages (or Spanish chorizo),
cut into 20 diagonal slices, 1.5 cm thick
10 cherry tomatoes, halved
3 sweet pointed red peppers, deseeded and
cut into 20 wedges (about 2cm square)
2 tablespoons olive oil
Cheddar cheese, grated
few basil leaves, chopped
sea salt and cracked black pepper

Lap-Cheong are Chinese dried sausages made from pork and pork fat with a savoury-sweet aroma. They are usually served wok-fried with slices of fresh garlic but I found that roasted they take on a divine crusty edge and they release a lot of their fat, making them a tad healthier. For a vegetarian version of these bites, substitute cubes of sweet potato and roast them with the peppers and tomatoes.

Preparation time: **5 minutes**          Cooking time: **10 minutes**

**1.** Preheat the oven to 220°C/425°F/Gas Mark 7.
**2.** Put the sausage slices on a small roasting tray and the cherry tomatoes and sweet pepper on a separate tray. Drizzle olive oil over the cherry tomatoes and sweet peppers and season with salt and pepper. Cook the cherry tomato and sweet peppers first for 10 minutes. Halfway through, put the sausages in the oven and cook for 5 minutes.
**3.** Remove both trays and pile the sausage pieces on top of the red pepper and the cherry tomatoes on top of the sausage in layers. Sprinkle cheese over the top and return to the oven for a few minutes to melt the cheese.
**4.** Transfer the bites to a serving dish and sprinkle with chopped basil. Serve immediately.

# Ketchup Prawns

serves 1

1 tablespoon groundnut oil
8 raw tiger prawns, heads off, deveined, shell and
tails on
8 tablespoons ketchup
1 tablespoon light soy sauce
1 spring onion, finely chopped

I always keep tiger prawns in my freezer so that after a busy day at work I can cook up a nutritious dinner without a trip to the supermarket. This recipe is a good cure for jetlag, too – one I 'invented' after a long flight home. Ravenous and tired, I could find only ketchup and frozen prawns. (To defrost, I run them under the cold tap then under warm water for a few minutes.) These are now known as my lazy yet tasty ketchup prawns. The ketchup reduces to a sticky sweet coating on the prawns: if you keep the shells on, they taste even better, but it's up to you.

Preparation time: **10 minutes**          Cooking time: **5 minutes**

**1.** Heat a wok over high heat and add the oil. Throw in the tiger prawns and stir fry until they turn pink. Add the ketchup and stir well; the sauce will reduce quickly so stir in the light soy sauce. Add the spring onions and give one last stir.
**2.** Eat them with your fingers or serve on a bed of Jasmine Rice (see page 142).

# Smoked Salmon and Crème Fraîche Spring Onion Wrap serves 2

8 slices smoked salmon (preferably oak-smoked
   wild Alaskan)
200ml crème fraîche
small bunch of chives, finely chopped
salt and freshly ground black pepper

for the flatbread (makes 4 large)
130g plain flour plus extra for kneading
2 pinches of salt
110ml hot water
dab of olive oil
1¹/₂ tablespoons toasted sesame oil
1 spring onion, finely chopped

4 tablespoons olive oil

In China, a national snack is Tsong-Yo Ping, which is spring onion flatbread. It can be served in many different ways, wrapped around a Chinese Mushroom Omelette, for example (see page 85). I'm a big fan of smoked salmon – especially the wild Alaskan variety, preferably oak smoked. Whichever variety you choose, a few slices on Tsong-Yo Ping with a dollop of crème fraîche and chopped chives makes an unforgettable appetiser or snack.

**Preparation: 20 minutes**          **Cooking time: 10 minutes**

**1.** For the flatbread, combine the flour and salt in a bowl, stir in the hot water and work into a dough. Turn out on a floured surface and knead for 5 minutes until the dough is smooth and elastic looking. Oil the surface with a little olive oil. Place in a floured bowl and cover with a damp tea towel and let it rest at room temperature for 20 minutes.

**2.** Take the dough and roll into a long roll then divide it into 4 equal pieces. Roll each one into a ball using the palm of your hand and then flatten out with a rolling pin into a small disc. Brush with sesame oil and sprinkle some finely chopped spring onion. Reform them into balls again then roll into flat discs about 3mm thick.

**3.** Heat a wok or pan over high heat, add 1 tablespoon of olive oil (no need to use any oil if you have a non-stick pan, just dry heat it); heat the flat dough until golden brown turning them over to cook them on both sides. Keep each one warm covered with foil while you make the rest.

**4.** Place 2 slices of salmon on each flatbread, top with crème fraîche and chives, season with salt and freshly ground black pepper, wrap up and enjoy.

# Mozzarella, Tomato and Basil Baked Wontons
# with Sun-dried Tomato Dip  makes 10

*30 mozzarella pearl balls (about 1cm diameter),*
  *drained well*
*12 tablespoons tinned chopped tomatoes, drained*
  *thoroughly and cut into 1cm cubes*
*about 30 basil leaves, freshly chopped*
*10 wonton wrappers*
*1 tablespoon olive oil*
*salt and freshly ground black pepper*

*10 chive strings*

for the sun-dried tomato dip
*5 sun-dried tomatoes, chopped*
*1 tablespoon balsamic vinegar*
*2 tablespoons extra virgin olive oil*
*salt and freshly ground black pepper*

When I lived in Milan during my student years, I was always amazed by the quality and standard of Italian food. By comparison, the Chinese food I had there was awful – too salty and far too oily. My friends and I always tried to eat out once a week at a wonderful local restaurant called Oca da Juiliva, otherwise known to us as 'The Duck Place'. Pizzas served with plenty of fresh mozzarella were just one of their many specialities – the seafood spaghetti was particularly good served with fresh langoustines. The owner would always double up the portions just for us and the complimentary frosty Limoncello was a hit too. After the exchange trip I was in love with everything Italian and thus this recipe was born. Crazy as it sounds, delicate little cheese wontons are fabulous – they just melt in the mouth.

Preparation: **10 minutes**          Cooking time: **10 minutes**

**1.** Preheat the oven to 200°C/400°F/Gas Mark 6.
**2.** Combine the mozzarella pearl balls, tinned tomatoes and basil and season well.
**3.** Take a wonton wrapper in your palm. Put a teaspoonful of the mozzarella mixture into the wonton. Make sure that there isn't any excess moisture in the mixture, or the wrapper will break. Dab a little of water on each corner of the wrapper then bring the corners to the centre and twist to seal the filling.
**4.** Grease a baking tray with the olive oil, transfer the parcels to the tray and bake for 5–6 minutes until golden brown.
**5.** Meanwhile, whizz all the ingredients for the dip in a food processor or blender.
**6.** When the wontons are cooked, transfer to a serving plate, tie some chive strings to the tops and serve immediately with the sun-dried tomato dip.

# Minced Lamb, Aubergine and Chilli Stuffed Roast Red Peppers

serves 4

*2 tablespoons groundnut oil*
*2 garlic cloves, finely chopped*
*1 tablespoon freshly grated ginger*
*300g minced lamb*
*¹/₂ aubergine, chopped into 1cm cubes*
*2 tablespoons shaosing rice wine or dry sherry*
*1 tablespoon garlic chilli sauce*
*1 tablespoon light soy sauce*
*2 pinches of salt and freshly ground black pepper*

*4 red peppers, tops cut across keeping stems*
    *intact, bases deseeded with a spoon*
*extra virgin olive oil*
*kalamata olives*

I love roasted vegetables, Mediterranean-style. I have been fortunate enough to taste the real thing in Italy during my student years so it's not surprising that my next best friend to my wok is my trusted oven.

To celebrate this my recipe fuses two cooking techniques: stir frying and roasting, East meeting West. The minced lamb and aubergine are stir fried and coated in delicious Chinese essential ingredients such as garlic, ginger and soy. The filling is then stuffed into the peppers and roasted until the peppers soften and release a little of their juices... the result is magic, a match made in culinary heaven. You can also make them with minced beef.

Preparation time: **10 minutes**          Cooking time: **20–25 minutes**

**1.** Preheat the oven to 200°C/400°F/Gas Mark 6.
**2.** Heat a wok over high heat and add the oil. When it is smoking, add the garlic and ginger and stir fry until slightly browned. Add the minced lamb and stir fry for less than 1 minute then add the aubergine and stir fry for less than 1 minute. Add the shaosing rice wine and stir well. Season with garlic chilli sauce, light soy, salt and freshly ground pepper.
**3.** Spoon the mixture into the red peppers, filling each one. Place the top of the pepper back on and ensure it fits snugly, otherwise the filling will dry out. Place the peppers on a baking tray and roast for 20 minutes until softened and slightly and browned.
**4.** To serve, place the peppers on a plate with a drizzle of extra virgin olive oil around it and a few kalamata olives.

# Guangdong Duck with Mango Salsa   serves 4

2 duck breasts, skin on

for the marinade
*¹/₂ teaspoon Chinese five-spice powder*
*1 tablespoon sesame oil*
*3 tablespoons hoi sin sauce*
*3 tablespoons brown sugar*
*3 tablespoons water*
*1 tablespoon dark soy sauce*

for the mango salsa
*3 tablespoons olive oil*
*¹/₂ teaspoon grated garlic*
*1 teaspoon freshly grated ginger*
*¹/₂ red onion, finely chopped*
*2 ripe mangoes, peeled, stoned, and diced*
*    into chunks*
*4 tablespoons lime juice*
*1 teaspoon soft brown sugar*
*1 teaspoon minced red chilli*
*6–8 mint leaves, shredded*
*pinch of sea salt and cracked black pepper*

*groundnut oil for deep frying*

to garnish
*4 mung bean noodle nests*
*fresh coriander leaves*

In my family, there is a general culinary rule never to mix meat with fruit in a dish. I was brought up with this rule and never really questioned it. However, I have since spread my wings and have discovered that meat accompanied with the 'right' fruit is a delight. This recipe fuses two of my favourite snacks: Peking duck and mango salsa. Thank goodness rules were made to be broken!

Preparation time: **10 minutes plus marinating**      Cooking time: **15 minutes**

**1.** Mix together all the marinade ingredients. Place the duck breasts into a ziplock plastic bag and pour in the marinade. Leave to marinate overnight.

**2.** Preheat the oven to 220°C/425°F/Gas Mark 7. Preheat a wok or pan (no oil) then brown the skin of the duck breasts, skin side down, for 1 minute until golden brown. Then place on a roasting tray and cook in the oven for about 15 minutes (the actual time will vary according to the size of the breasts and how rare you prefer your meat). At this temperature, it will be well done.

**3.** Prepare the mango salsa by thoroughly mixing all the ingredients in a bowl.

**4.** In a wok or pan, heat the oil and deep fry 4 mung bean noodle nests until crispy and opaque white in colour. Remove and drain on kitchen paper.

**5.** When the duck is cooked, slice it into bite-sized pieces. Arrange the pieces on a nest of mung bean noodles. Garnish with fresh coriander and serve with the mango salsa in a dipping bowl.

# Chinese Mushroom Omelette with Salad and Soy Dressing serves 1

2 eggs, beaten
2 dried Chinese mushrooms, soaked in hot
    water for 20 minutes, stems discarded,
    finely chopped
1/2 spring onion, finely chopped
sesame oil
1 tablespoon olive oil
salt and freshly ground white pepper

100g mixed salad leaves (escarole, lollo rosso,
    lamb's lettuce)
3 cherry tomatoes, halved

for the soy dressing
1 tablespoon cider vinegar
1 tablespoon light soy sauce
2 tablespoons extra virgin olive oil
1/2 teaspoon soft brown sugar
pinch of salt and freshly ground black pepper

Chinese dried shiitake mushrooms are a must in any kitchen, in my opinion. They are fabulously fragrant with a woody, earthy aroma. They need to be rehydrated – just immerse them in hot water and let them soak for about 20 minutes. This simple omelette recipe is perfect for brunch or as a shared starter or snack. For another East/West twist, the salad dressing fuses light soy, cider vinegar and olive oil.

Preparation: **10 minutes**       Cooking time: **8 minutes**

**1.** Mix the eggs, mushrooms, spring onion, sesame oil, salt and pepper in a bowl.
**2.** Heat a wok or pan over high heat, add the olive oil and swirl the oil around.
**3.** Pour the mixture into the wok, swirling it around until it coats the wok evenly and thinly roughly the size of a dinner plate. Let the omelette brown on one side and then turn or flip it over on the other side. Reduce the heat once cooked but leave the pan on the hob to keep warm.
**4.** Put all the dressing ingredients in a bowl and whisk well.
**5.** Slide the omelette onto a plate and fold in half. Serve with the mixed salad and cherry tomatoes drizzled with the soy dressing.

# Peking Duck and Marmalade Sandwich serves 1

hoi sin sauce
marmalade
2 slices of crusty white bread
50g shredded Peking duck (see page 60)
baby spinach leaves
1/2 spring onion, green part only, finely chopped

Mmm... here is a delicious snack made using leftover Peking duck, which I usually serve instead of turkey at Christmas. Inspired by turkey, stuffing and cranberry sandwiches, I thought to try Peking duck and marmalade, two of the best inventions and representations of East and West. You will either love this one or not. But I hope it's love.

Preparation: **5 minutes**

**1.** Spread a layer of hoi sin on one slice of bread and marmalade on the other. Sprinkle the Peking duck on one slice then add some spinach leaves and the spring onion. Place the other slice on top, cut in half and enjoy!

# Mock Duck and Asparagus Stir Fry   serves 4

2 tablespoons groundnut oil

1 garlic clove, crushed and finely chopped

1 tablespoon grated ginger

1 red chilli, deseeded and sliced

4 dried Chinese mushrooms, soaked in hot water
    for 20 minutes, drained, sliced, stem discarded

190g tinned mock duck, drained

100g baby asparagus spears

100g French beans

2 tablespoons oyster sauce

1 tablespoon fish sauce (nam pla)

1 tablespoon soft brown sugar

pinch of ground black pepper (optional)

dash of toasted sesame oil

In the Far East it's very popular to be vegetarian and if you are, it's 'vegetarian heaven' out there because they have all sorts of delicious ingredients made with soya and gluten, ranging from vegetarian sausages, mock chicken and mock fish – including tuna and swordfish varieties! It's all quite mind-blowing with the tastes and textures just like the real thing. There are also varieties of dried, fresh and fermented beancurds. Some oriental supermarkets in the UK import tinned mock meats such as mock duck and they make a great ingredient in a stir fry. This is one such recipe made with fresh asparagus and French beans.

Preparation time: **5 minutes**          Cooking time: **5 minutes**

**1.** Heat a wok over high heat and add the groundnut oil. Add the garlic, ginger, chilli and Chinese mushrooms and stir fry for 1 minute. Add the mock duck and stir fry for less than 1 minute. Add the asparagus and French beans and stir fry for less than 1 minute.

**2.** Season with oyster sauce, fish sauce, sugar, black pepper (if using) and sesame oil.

**3.** Serve with steamed Jasmine Rice and Steamed Gai Lan and Garlic Oyster Sauce (see pages 142 and 144).

# Soba Noodles with Olives, Sun-dried Tomatoes and Rice Vinegar Dressing   serves 2

120g dried soba noodles
few dashes of sesame oil
1 tablespoon groundnut oil
1 garlic clove, crushed and finely chopped
5 dried Chinese mushrooms, soaked in hot water
    for 20 minutes, drained, sliced, stem discarded
6 sun-dried tomatoes, sliced
10 black olives, pitted

for the rice vinegar dressing
2 tablespoons toasted sesame oil
2 tablespoons rice vinegar or mirin
2 tablespoons light soy sauce

to serve
3 tablespoons toasted sesame seeds
handful shredded mint leaves or rocket leaves

This is a recipe that pays tribute to the Chinese cook, the Japanese inventor and the Italian farmer. It was proved recently through archaeological records that the Chinese were the first to invent wheatflour noodles. The Japanese invented the soba (buckwheat) noodle and the Italians brought to us delicious sun-dried tomatoes and olives (well, not only the Italians, of course; we have all the Mediterranean countries to thank for these wonderful ingredients, but the Italians know how to combine them with their own style of 'noodle'). This is a gorgeously simple recipe that fuses East and West – the results are scrumptious.

Preparation time: **5 minutes**         Cooking time: **2 minutes**

1. Cook the noodles according to the instructions on the packet, drain and refresh under cold water, then add a few dashes of sesame oil to stop them sticking, and set aside.
2. Heat a wok over high heat and add the groundnut oil. Add the garlic and mushrooms and stir fry for 1 minute, or until the mushrooms are cooked.
3. Combine all the ingredients for the rice vinegar dressing in a bowl and mix well.
4. To serve, place the noodles in a bowl, add the mushrooms, the sun-dried tomatoes and olives. Mix well and pour over the rice vinegar dressing. Sprinkle with sesame seeds and the shredded mint or rocket leaves. The dish is best kept refrigerated and served chilled.

# Eastern-style Tuna Salade Niçoise   serves 2

2 tuna steaks
100g French beans
2 eggs
olive oil
200g mixed leaf salad, washed and shredded
8 cherry tomatoes
2 teaspoons capers, rinsed and drained
8 kalamata olives
2 teaspoons fresh salmon roe

for the marinade
1 tablespoon freshly grated ginger
1 tablespoon light soy sauce
1 tablespoon shaosing rice wine or dry sherry
1 tablespoon mirin
dash of sesame oil
pinch of salt and freshly ground black pepper

for the dressing
1 teaspoon wasabi paste
juice of 1 lemon
5 tablespoons extra virgin olive oil
pinch of salt and freshly ground black pepper

In my salad company, we are always experimenting with new salad recipes. This is my Eastern-style Salade Niçoise. Tuna steaks are marinated in a light ginger, soy and rice wine marinade, pan fried and then served on a bed of mixed leaves with all the trimmings: crunchy French beans, hard-boiled egg, Kalamata olives, capers, cherry tomatoes and salmon roe. Instead of a French vinegar dressing, a delicious and light dressing made with a hint of wasabi (Japanese horseradish) lifts the salad and gives it a mild and addictive kick. This is a fabulously healthy recipe.

Preparation time: **10 minutes plus marinating**          Cooking time: **10 minutes**

**1.** Combine all the marinade ingredients in a bowl and marinate the tuna steaks for as long as possible.

**2.** Blitz the dressing ingredients in a food processor or blender.

**3.** Bring a pan of salted water to the boil and blanch the French beans. Drain and refresh under cold running water.

**4.** In another small pan of boiling water, boil the eggs for about 5 minutes. Plunge into cold water then peel and quarter when cold.

**5.** Heat a griddle pan, drizzle with a little olive oil and cook the tuna steaks for 2 minutes on one side then turn and cook the other side.

**6.** Layer the mixed leaf salad, cherry tomatoes, boiled eggs and French beans on 2 plates.

**7.** Place the tuna steak on top, and sprinkle with capers, olives and the salmon roe. Drizzle generously with dressing and serve immediately.

# Tiger Prawns Provençale-style Rice Noodles serves 6

200g dried vermicelli rice noodles

for the sauce
2 tablespoons olive oil
1 large onion, peeled and chopped
1 garlic clove, crushed and finely chopped
2 courgettes, sliced 1cm thick
6 large tomatoes, skinned and chopped
200ml tinned plum tomatoes
400ml vegetable stock
1 tablespoon tomato purée
2 teaspoons dried mixed herbs (rosemary,
    tarragon, parsley)
12 raw tiger prawns, shelled and deveined
salt and freshly ground black pepper

A tomato-based Provence-inspired sauce that makes a healthy delicious supper: simple and satisfying. I like to serve this with vermicelli rice noodles, which complement the sauce well, soaking up all its flavours. The overall meal isn't too heavy either. It is a quick dinner favourite – perfect with a glass of white wine.

Preparation: **10 minutes**          Cooking time: **20 minutes**

1. Cook the noodles according to the instructions on the packet, drain then rinse under cold water and set aside.
2. Heat a wok or pan over high heat and add the oil. Throw in the onions and garlic and fry gently until the onions are transparent. Add the courgettes, tomatoes, stock, purée and herbs and cook for 20 minutes stirring occasionally. Add the tiger prawns, cook for a further 2 minutes, and season with salt and pepper.
3. Refresh the noodles with boiling water from the kettle, drain then share out onto serving plates. Distribute the prawns, vegetables and sauce over the noodles. Serve immediately.

# Steamed Plaice Fillets in Banana Leaves with Mustard Caper Sauce serves 2

2 plaice fillets, rinsed and patted dry
2 pieces of banana leaf, washed
juice of 1 lime
salt and freshly ground black pepper

for the mustard caper sauce
knob of butter
1 onion, chopped
2 yellow peppers, deseeded and chopped
1 tablespoon prepared English mustard
150ml white wine
1 tablespoon rice vinegar
small handful of capers, plus extra to garnish
salt and freshly ground black pepper

Another Mediterranean-style fish recipe, served Chinese style in banana leaves. They make a real difference, adding flavour and helping to keep the fish tender and moist. The rice vinegar lends an Eastern tang. If you cannot get banana leaves, you can do without and wrap the fish in foil.

Preparation: **10 minutes**          Cooking time: **15 minutes**

1. Put the plaice fillets on the banana leaves, season with salt and pepper, drizzle with lime juice then wrap the fillets in the leaves, securing with toothpicks. Place the parcels on a heatproof plate that fits in a bamboo steamer. Fill a wok or pan with boiling water to a depth that will not submerge the base of the steamer and steam the parcels for 10 minutes.
2. Heat another wok or pan over high heat, add the butter and sauté the onions and peppers until softened. Add the mustard, white wine, rice vinegar, capers and salt and pepper.
3. Blitz the sauce ingredients in a food processor or blender to make a thick sauce.
4. Transfer the plaice to a plate, drizzle with sauce and extra capers. Serve with steamed rice.

# Chinese-style Fish and Chips   serves 2

2 x 170g whole cod fillets, about 2.5cm thick
groundnut oil for deep frying
2 large potatoes, cut into chunky-sized chips
plain flour

for the marinade
2 teaspoons shaosing rice wine or dry sherry
1 tablespoon freshly grated ginger
1 spring onion, finely chopped
salt
ground white pepper

for the batter
50g plain flour
1/2 teaspoon baking powder
100ml water
1 teaspoon groundnut oil

for the chilli ketchup
1 tablespoon Sweet Chilli Jam (see page 142)
2 tablespoons ketchup

Every Friday at school we had fish and chips on the menu. Although not very healthy, I looked forward to it with a passion. Nothing beats crisp chunky homemade chips and of course homemade batter makes all the difference too, especially with some baking powder added to make the batter rise. I like to marinate the cod with some shaosing rice wine (which gives it a sweet edge), ginger and spring onion for as long as possible.

Preparation: **15 minutes plus marinating**          Cooking time: **30 minutes**

**1.** Marinate the fish in the marinade ingredients for as long as possible, overnight is best.
**2.** For the batter, combine the flour, baking powder, water and mix well. Then stir in the groundnut oil and leave to stand for 1 hour.
**3.** In a small pan combine the chilli jam and ketchup. Set aside.
**4.** Heat a wok and add enough oil for deep frying (about 350ml). Heat to 180°C/350°F or until a small piece of bread turns golden brown in 15 seconds. Be careful when deep frying in a wok. Place the chips in a colander and rinse under cold water then pat really dry with kitchen paper. Deep fry the chips in batches for about 3–4 minutes until golden brown. Then drain any excess oil from the chips on kitchen paper and keep warm.
**5.** Remove the cod from the marinade and sprinkle some flour over the fillets, shake off any excess and dip into the batter and deep fry for 3-4 minutes until golden brown. Drain any excess oil on kitchen paper.
**6.** Serve with chunky chips and chilli ketchup.

# Pan-fried Scallops with Crisp Parma Ham, Asparagus and Herby Salsa Verde serves 2

12 baby asparagus spears
2 tablespoons olive oil
8 scallops, cleaned, debearded, coral removed if
  preferred, washed and dried on kitchen paper
8 slices Parma ham
salt and freshly cracked black pepper

for the herby salsa verde
bunch of coriander
bunch of mint
bunch of basil
1 tablespoon extra virgin olive oil
juice of 1 lime
1 teaspoon brown sugar
1 teaspoon freshly grated ginger

If you have a good local fishmonger, there's nothing more impressive than sweet, pan-fried fresh scallops as a main or as a starter. I love the Chinese style of cooking scallops, steamed in bamboo baskets with a dash of soy and ginger dressing – very minimalist, very delicious. However, for the East–West theme, I thought to try pan-fried scallops with crispy Parma ham, blanched asparagus and salsa verde on the side. The asparagus and the salsa provide a delicate herby accompaniment and the Parma ham delivers an unforgettable smoky flavour and texture.

Preparation: **5 minutes**        Cooking time: **10 minutes**

1. Blanch the asparagus in a pan of boiling water for 3 minutes until al dente. Drain and run under cold water to stop them cooking. Set aside.
2. Blitz all the ingredients for the salsa in a food processor or blender. Set aside.
3. Heat a large flat-based pan and add the olive oil. Season the scallops with a little salt and freshly cracked black pepper and cook on one side until they start to turn opaque white. Use a palette knife to turn them over and cook for about 2 minutes – they should be browned on both sides.
4. Place the Parma ham slices in the side of the pan; they will crisp in no time. Reduce the heat but leave the pan on the hob.
5. Refresh the asparagus with boiling water from the kettle and drain. Season with salt and cracked black pepper. Divide the spears between 2 plates, add a layer of crisp Parma ham and place the scallops on top. Drizzle some of the herby salsa around the edges of the plate and serve immediately.

# Chinese-style Seafood Risotto  serves 2–4

1 litre fish stock

2 tablespoons olive oil

$^1/_2$ onion diced

2 garlic cloves, crushed and chopped

2 bay leaves, torn in half

6 fresh shiitake mushrooms

200g arborio (risotto) rice

2 tablespoons shaosing rice wine or dry sherry

14 mussels, cleaned and debearded (discard any
    that remain open when tapped)

8 raw tiger prawns, shelled and deveined,
    tails on

100g salmon fillet, about 5cm thick, cut into
    even-sized chunks

sesame oil

1 tablespoon freshly chopped coriander

1 tablespoon freshly chopped spring onion

salt and freshly ground black pepper

When I was studying in Milan, I was introduced to some of the best risottos and my favourite was always the one with lots of fresh seafood. I think risottos are similar to the Chinese Xi-fan (see page 52), although Xi-fan is a lot more watery and isn't cooked in the same way as risotto. This is my Chinese-style seafood risotto. I add fresh shiitake mushrooms, shaosing rice wine and plenty of coriander in this Eastern variation: it is subtle yet discernably tasty.

**Preparation time: 5 minutes**          **Cooking time: 35 minutes**

**1.** Pour the stock into a large pan and bring to a simmer.

**2.** Heat a large pan and add the olive oil. Fry the onion, garlic, bay leaves and shiitake mushrooms and sauté for a few minutes. Stir in the rice and add the fish stock a ladle at a time, stirring and adding more stock as each batch of stock is absorbed. (It's important to keep the stock simmering.) Keep cooking in this way for about 20 minutes until the rice is al dente.

**3.** Put the shaosing rice wine in another pan and cook the mussels until they open. Discard any unopened ones.

**4.** Stir the prawns and salmon fillets into the rice and cook for 2 minutes. Keep stirring and adding more stock if the rice is dry or sticking to the base. Discard the bay leaves.

**5.** Season the risotto with sesame oil, coriander, spring onion, salt and pepper.

**6.** Ladle into 2 bowls, add the mussels on top and serve immediately.

# Chicken and Shiitake Mushroom Pies   serves 4

knob of butter
*¹/₂ onion, diced*
*50g frozen peas*
*6 fresh shiitake mushrooms, sliced around the*
*    stem, stems discarded*
*300g poached chicken breast, shredded*
*300g chicken stock*
*150ml double cream*
*¹/₂ teaspoon dried tarragon leaves*
*generous pinch of Chinese five-spice powder*
*2 pinches of salt and a pinch of freshly cracked*
*    black pepper*

*2 sheets puff pastry*
*1 beaten egg*

*4 x 10cm circular pie dishes*

What seems like an honest simple chicken and mushroom pie has hidden Chinese delights. Shiitake mushrooms are the twist, along with Chinese five-spice powder. What seems familiar has just a hint of the exotic and it tastes good! I find this real comfort food and if I were ever to relocate to the depths of China, I could take this recipe with me and re-create it and perhaps open up a chain of pubs....

Preparation time: **10 minutes**          Cooking time: **30 minutes**

**1.** Preheat the oven to 180°C/350°F/Gas Mark 4.
**2.** Heat a wok or pan over high heat. Add the butter and stir fry the onion until slightly translucent, then add the peas and mushrooms and stir fry for less than 1 minute. Add the shredded chicken and the stock and stir well. Pour in the double cream, add the tarragon and season with five-spice powder, salt and cracked black pepper. Set aside.
**3.** Roll out the pastry to about 3mm thick. Use a pie dish as a template to cut out enough pastry to line the bases of the dishes as well as make 4 tops. Line the dishes with the pastry then share out the pie filling, top with a circle of pastry and glaze with beaten egg.
**4.** Bake for 25 minutes until the pastry is risen and golden. Serve with Green Salad and Oriental Dressing (see page 147).

# Lemon Honey Turkey Escalopes   serves 2

*2 turkey escalopes*
*sprig of rosemary, freshly chopped*
*50g plain flour*
*1 egg, beaten*
*50g dried breadcrumbs*
*4 tablespoons groundnut oil*
*salt and freshly ground black pepper*

for the lemon sauce
*juice of 2 lemons*
*3 tablespoons honey*
*pinch of cinnamon*
*1 teaspoon cornflour blended with*
*    2 teaspoons water*

At first glance, most of the ingredients in this recipe may seem more western than eastern but the lemon sauce is a creation inspired by the classic lemon chicken dish found in many Chinese takeaways and restaurants. This recipe is delicious, healthy and satisfying. You'll enjoy serving it time and time again.

Preparation: **10 minutes**          Cooking time: **10 minutes**

**1.** Season the escalopes with salt and pepper and sprinkle with rosemary. Coat each escalopes first in flour, then in egg and finally in breadcrumbs.
**2.** Heat a frying pan over medium heat and add the oil. Fry the escalopes for 10 minutes, turning once.
**3.** Put the lemon juice, honey and cinnamon in a small pan and bring to the boil. Stir in the blended cornflour to thicken the sauce.
**4.** Serve the escalopes on blanched green beans with the lemon honey sauce drizzled over.

# Oriental-style Meatballs and Spicy Coconut Noodles     serves 2

for the meatballs

*350g minced beef*

*4 garlic cloves, crushed and finely chopped*

*1 tablespoon freshly grated ginger*

*1 medium red chilli, deseeded and finely chopped*

*4 tablespoons coriander, finely chopped*

*1 large spring onion, finely chopped*

*2 tablespoons shaosing rice wine or dry sherry*

*2 tablespoons fish sauce (nam pla)*

*1 teaspoon toasted sesame oil*

*1 egg yolk*

*1/2 teaspoon salt*

*pinch of freshly ground black pepper*


*6 tablespoons groundnut oil*


for the coconut noodles

*160g dried, flat udon (wheatflour) noodles*

*1 tablespoon toasted sesame oil*

*1 tablespoon groundnut oil*

*2 garlic cloves, crushed and finely chopped*

*1 tablespoon freshly grated ginger*

*1 medium red chilli, deseeded and finely chopped*

*1 lemongrass stalk, outer leaves discarded,*
   *finely chopped*

*1 tablespoon shrimp paste*

*400ml coconut milk*

*1–2 tablespoons fish sauce (nam pla)*

*2 spring onions, finely chopped*

*4 tablespoons finely chopped coriander*

This is my oriental version of spaghetti meatballs. The meatballs are seasoned with garlic, ginger, chillies, coriander, spring onion and fish sauce. Pungent fish sauce is used mostly in Thai and Vietnamese cuisines, especially salads. Once cooked, however, its salty, fishy aroma takes on a sweet edge. The delicious coconut noodles are a great accompaniment.

Preparation time: **15 minutes**          Cooking time: **20 minutes**

1. Bring a large pan of salted water to the boil and cook the udon noodles according to the packet instructions, drain then refresh with cold running water to keep them springy. Add a few dashes of sesame oil to keep them from sticking, and set aside.

2. Put all the ingredients for the meatballs in a bowl and mix well. Form into 12 small meatballs.

3. Heat a wok over high heat, add the groundnut oil and shallow fry the meatballs for about 7 minutes until cooked through and browned on all sides (you may need to work in batches).

4. Remove with a slotted spoon and drain the meatballs on kitchen paper. Place them on a plate, cover with foil and keep warm.

5. Wipe out the wok with kitchen paper, reheat over high heat and add 1 tablespoon groundnut oil, stir fry the garlic, ginger and chilli for less than a minute. Stir in the lemongrass and shrimp paste then add the coconut milk and bring to the boil.

6. Mix in the cooked noodles, season with fish sauce and sprinkle over the spring onions and most of the coriander.

7. Return the meatballs to the wok, mixing carefully to avoid breaking them up and coat well with the sauce. Serve sprinkled with the remaining fresh coriander.

# Chicken, Beetroot and Mango Salad with Date, Soy and Balsamic Dressing serves 2

120g mixed salad leaves

2 large semi-ripe mangoes, finely sliced into long
    strips (preferably with a mandolin)

4 cooked beetroots, finely sliced into long strips
    (preferably with a mandolin)

80g enoki mushrooms or beansprouts

2 poached chicken breasts, shredded

for the dressing

2 tablespoons extra virgin olive oil

2 tablespoons light soy sauce

2 tablespoons balsamic vinegar

4 dates, stoned

2 tablespoons water

2 teaspoons soft brown sugar

I have what I call 'low days', days where nothing is cheerful. On such occasions, only three things can lift me from the spell: chocolate (momentary happiness then regret), shopping (short-lived cheer then guilt), and phone calls to girlfriends (or anyone willing to lend an ear). Failing that, some homemade Chicken, Beetroot and Mango Salad. If this fruity, punchy salad doesn't cheer you up, then call me! (If you are vegetarian, substitute crunchy roasted walnuts for the chicken.)

Preparation time: 10 minutes

**1.** Assemble the salad in layers, beginning with the leaves, then the mangoes, beetroots, enoki mushrooms and finally top with the chicken breast.

**2.** Whizz all the dressing ingredients in a blender, pour over the salad and serve.

# Lemon Chicken Burger with Roasted Sweet Potato Chips and Sweet Chilli Ketchup  serves 2

300g chicken breast, diced finely
2 large spring onions, finely chopped
1 teaspoon lemon juice
1 teaspoon rice wine
1 teaspoon cornflour
1 teaspoon soft brown sugar
dash of light soy sauce
dash of toasted sesame oil
salt and freshly ground black pepper
2 tablespoons olive oil

for the sweet potato chips
200g sweet potato, peeled and cut into chips
3 tablespoons olive oil
salt and freshly ground black pepper

for the sweet chilli ketchup
2 tablespoons Sweet Chilli Jam (see page 142)
2 tablespoons ketchup

to serve
2 sesame seed buns, grilled
4 tablespoons mayonnaise
2–4 Little Gem lettuce leaves
1 beef tomato, sliced

The first chicken burger I had was at the age of six, at the Tom Newby Primary School in South Africa, when my family moved there in 1984. I remember vividly being in the playground, unable to speak a word of English, with a girl I knew by the name of Lindsay who was assigned by the teachers to look after me. Lindsay bought me the burger for lunch and it was the most satisfying experience I had. The school had a great tuck shop where we bought our food if we didn't have packed lunches. My parents would give me five rand pocket money each week and I spent it on wonderful treats such as hot dogs, hot minced beef and ketchup toasted sandwiches, Nutella (which came in little plastic tubs, so we could eat it straight from the tub), marshmallows and jelly babies! All these foods were new to me, just as my brother and I were new to all the other children, many of whom had never before seen Chinese people. I have fond memories of South Africa and many of my first Western food memories are from there. The children knew how to throw great swimming pool and 'Braai' (barbecue) parties and chicken burgers were always popular. This is my Eastern chicken burger recipe.

**Preparation time: 10 minutes**     **Cooking time: 30 minutes**

**1.** Preheat the oven to 180°C/350°F/Gas Mark 4.
**2.** Put the prepared sweet potatoes on a baking tray, drizzle with olive oil, season with salt and pepper and put in the oven for 30–40 minutes.
**3.** Mix all the chicken burger ingredients in a bowl and shape into 2 large burger patties.
**4.** Heat a large griddle pan, drizzle with olive oil and place the chicken burgers on the pan and cook them on one side until the chicken turns opaque white. Then flip over to cook on the other side. Cook for about 8–10 minutes on medium heat.
**5.** Meanwhile make the Sweet Chilli Jam (see page 142). Once cooled slightly, mix 2 tablespoons of jam with 2 tablespoons of tomato ketchup in a dipping bowl.
**6.** To serve, slice the sesame buns, place them on the griddle to brown a little, then spread mayonnaise on the bun slices and divide the lettuce and tomato between the bottom halves. Put the chicken burger on top with a dollop of the sweet chilli ketchup and replace the top halves of the buns. Serve with the sweet potato chips.

# Taiwanese-style Chicken Caesar Salad  serves 2

2 x 100g skinless chicken breasts, cut into strips
1 tablespoon sea salt
1 tablespoon crushed dried red chilli flakes
1 egg yolk, beaten
3 tablespoons potato flour
100g Panko breadcrumbs
250ml sunflower oil, for pan frying
200g Cos lettuce, washed and shredded
12 cherry tomatoes
50g croûtons
16g Parmesan shavings
60g ready-made Caesar dressing

for the marinade
1 tablespoon ginger, grated
1 tablespoon light soy sauce
1 teaspoon oyster sauce
1 teaspoon ketchup
1 teaspoon yellow bean sauce
2 teaspoons sesame oil

I love Caesar salad with all the trimmings, the crispy croûtons, the crunchy cos lettuce, in fact everything has texture and crunch except the chicken. That's when I decided this recipe needed a makeover. My Taiwanese version sees the chicken marinated in light soy, yellow bean sauce, oyster sauce and more – it's then coated in Panko breadcrumbs (Japanese breadcrumbs) and shallow fried for a crispy coating. The chicken strips are delicious served warm over the cold salad. Naughty but amazingly tasty. The marinade is usually used in Taiwan to make fried pork cutlet (Zah Pai Gu). Served with rice (Zah Pai Gu Fan), it is a lunchbox bento (Pian-Dang) favourite with city professionals in Taipei.

**Preparation time: 40 minutes plus marinating**　　　　**Cooking time: 10 minutes**

**1.** Mix all the ingredients for the marinade. Place the chicken in a dish, pour over the marinade and leave it to marinate for as long as possible, overnight is best.

**2.** Season the chicken with sea salt and chilli flakes, then coat the breasts in egg yolk and lightly dredge with potato flour then smother with breadcrumbs.

**3.** Heat a wok over high heat and add the oil. Shallow-fry the chicken over a moderate heat for about 10 minutes, until cooked through and golden brown. Drain any excess oil on kitchen paper.

**4.** To assemble the salad, divide the cos lettuce and cherry tomatoes between 2 plates. Place the chicken on top, sprinkle with croûtons and Parmesan shavings, drizzle Caesar dressing generously over the top and serve immediately.

# Peking Duck Fillet with Savoy Cabbage, Roast Potatoes and Peking Duck Sauce serves 2

2 duck fillets
2 large round potatoes, peeled and thinly sliced
olive oil
pinch of mixed spice (cinnamon, coriander seed,
    caraway, nutmeg, ginger, cloves)
knob of butter
100g Savoy cabbage, shredded into lengths
salt and freshly ground black pepper

for the marinade
4 teaspoons clear honey
2 teaspoons dark soy sauce
2 teaspoons Chinese five-spice powder
2 teaspoons brown sugar
2 teaspoons plum wine

for the Peking duck sauce
2 tablespoons sesame oil
6 tablespoons hoi sin sauce
6 tablespoons caster sugar
6 tablespoons water
1 tablespoon dark soy sauce
1 tablespoon cornflour blended with 2 tablespoons
    cold water

1 spring onion, sliced lengthways, to garnish

This dish is perfect for a romantic dinner for two. It does take some time to prepare but it's worth it. This is also Peking duck with a twist. Roast potatoes and creamy Savoy cabbage in butter provide the Western edge in this recipe and make a great accompaniment to the duck. You can use duck leg instead of breast fillet. Duck can be a bit fatty but cooking it on the rack in a roasting tray will help the fat drip away.

**Preparation time: 30 minutes plus marinating**          **Cooking time: 1 hour**

**1.** Place the duck fillets on a rack over a roasting tin and pour over 500ml boiling water. Discard the water and pat dry the fillets with kitchen paper.

**2.** Mix together the ingredients for the marinade in a shallow dish and marinate the duck fillets for as long as possible: the longer they marinate the better the flavour, so ideally overnight in the fridge. The marinade should dry and glaze over the fillets because of the brown sugar. Keep brushing the marinade over and over the fillets until all the sauce is used.

**3.** When you are ready to cook the duck, preheat the oven to 200°C/400°F/Gas Mark 6. Place the prepared potatoes on a baking tray, drizzle a small amount of olive oil, season with a good pinch of mixed spice, salt and freshly ground pepper. Transfer the tray to the oven.

**4.** Place the duck fillets on the rack over a roasting tin and cook for 10 minutes, then turn them over and cook for a further 10 minutes until the skin is crisp. (You need to monitor the cooking time as it depends on how large the fillets are.) Turn the oven off and leave the duck in the oven while you prepare the other ingredients. The roast potatoes should be cooked by this time.

**5.** Heat a wok over high heat, melt the butter, add the Savoy cabbage and stir fry lightly until slightly tender, then season with a pinch of salt and freshly ground black pepper. Place it on a dish and cover with tinfoil and put in the oven to keep warm.

**6.** To make the sauce, wipe the wok down with kitchen paper; reheat and add the sesame oil. Stir in the rest of the sauce ingredients except the cornflour. Bring the sauce to the boil and stir in the blended cornflour.

**7.** To serve, assemble 3 slices of roast potatoes on 2 large plates, add a layer of Savoy cabbage, then another layer of potatoes and another layer of Savoy cabbage. Place the Peking duck fillet on top. Drizzle the sauce around the plate, garnish with the spring onion and serve.

# Char Siu Pork with Caramelised Onions, Roast Parsnips and Char Siu Gravy serves 2

1 x 500g pork fillet

for the marinade
2 garlic cloves, crushed and finely chopped
2 tablespoons freshly grated ginger
50ml light soy sauce
50ml shaosing rice wine
3 tablespoons soft brown sugar
2 tablespoons yellow bean sauce
1 tablespoon hoi sin sauce
1 tablespoon groundnut oil
60ml honey
1 spring onion, sliced lengthways
salt and freshly ground black pepper

for the roast parsnips
400g parsnips
2 tablespoons olive oil
1 small handful of fresh or dried thyme
salt and freshly ground black pepper

for the caramelised onions
25g butter
4 medium red onions, thinly sliced
1 tablespoon soft brown sugar
1 tablespoon apricot brandy or brandy
1/2 teaspoon salt
1/2 teaspoon freshly ground pepper

If you are having Chinese and English guests round, this recipe is guaranteed to satisfy both parties. The familiarity of French-style caramelised onions with roasted parsnips and steamed Brussels sprouts fused with delicious Char Siu roast pork fillet and Char Siu gravy makes this unique and full of flavour. It can also make a wonderful change from the usual Sunday roast dinner, and why not indeed? In fact why not try this recipe instead of turkey at Christmas?

Preparation time: **12 minutes plus marinating**     Cooking time: **40 minutes**

**1.** Make slashes in the sides of the pork fillet. Combine all the ingredients for the marinade and marinate the pork for a few hours or for as long as possible, overnight is best.

**2.** Preheat the oven to 200°C/400°F/Gas Mark 6.

**3.** Remove the pork from the marinade and place on a rack in a roasting tin. Pour water into the tin to come half way up the sides. Roast the fillet for 20 minutes then turn it over and baste with some of the remaining marinade (reserve the rest). Reduce the temperature to 180°C/350°F/Gas Mark 4 and cook for a further 20 minutes.

**4.** At this stage, put the parsnips in a second roasting tray, drizzle with olive oil and season with thyme, salt and pepper and put in the oven.

**5.** Heat a wok over high heat and add the butter. Throw in the red onions and cook until softened, add the brown sugar and mix well until caramelised. Add the brandy and season with salt and black pepper.

**6.** Put the reserved marinade into another small pan and bring to the boil.

**7.** Once the pork is cooked, slice and serve with the parsnips and caramelised onions with plenty of the Char Siu gravy drizzled over. It's also delicious with steamed Chinese broccoli (see page 144) or Brussels sprouts.

# Lychee and Mango Trifle  serves 4

450g Madeira cake, ready bought

1 tin lychees, drained unless you are not
   using liqueur

400g fresh mangoes, sliced

5 tablespoons Grand Marnier (optional)

400g ready-made custard

1 pint whipping cream

prepared fresh strawberries, lychees and mangoes
   to decorate

An easy dessert that is delicious and refreshing after a heavy supper. I regularly make this dessert because it's fast, unfussy and simple to make, especially for a crowd. It is a firm favourite with children, too (minus the alcohol). Lychees and mangoes pair very well and the Grand Marnier adds a special flavour.

Preparation time: **20 minutes plus 1 hour chilling**

**1.** Slice the Madeira cake and fit it in the bottom of a trifle dish. Top with a layer of lychees and mangoes over the cake and add a drizzle of Grand Marnier or some juice from the lychee tin. Add another layer of cake, more Grand Marnier or juice and more fruit. Top with a layer of custard.

**2.** Whip the cream until it forms soft peaks. Smooth a layer over the top of the trifle and refrigerate for 1 hour.

**3.** Just before you are ready to serve, decorate with strawberries, more lychees and mangoes.


# Scones with Blueberry and Lychee Compôte  makes 6

250g self-raising flour

pinch of salt

50g margarine

50g caster sugar

150ml milk

1 egg, beaten, for glazing

for the compôte

175g blueberries

150g lychees, drained if using tinned

100g caster sugar

1 tablespoon water

2 tablespoons apricot brandy or brandy

whipped cream

Not quite a dessert, more of a tea-time afternoon treat. The lychees give this very English recipe a modern Chinese twist. I'm a great fan of French-style compôtes, too, and I think they make a delicious change from strawberry jam.

Preparation time: **20 minutes plus 1–2 hours chilling**   Cooking time: **25 minutes**

**1.** Preheat the oven to 220°C/450°F/Gas Mark 7. Sift the flour and salt in bowl. Rub in the margarine with your fingers to make fine breadcrumbs. Stir in the caster sugar and enough milk to make a soft but not sticky dough.

**2.** Turn out the dough onto a floured surface and knead lightly. Roll it out until it is 1cm thick. Use a 5cm round cutter to stamp out 12 rounded pieces of the dough. Pile one piece on top of another so they stick together. Place on a lightly floured baking tray and brush the top with a beaten egg. Bake for 15 minutes until golden brown and well risen. Leave to cool on a wire rack.

**3.** To make the compôte, heat the blueberries, lychees and sugar in a small pan, adding the water if the fruit starts to catch. Add the apricot brandy and stir until the sugar melts. Remove from the heat, allow to cool then chill the compôte in the fridge for 1-2 hours.

**4.** Cut the scones in half, spread with cream and top with compôte. Serve... with English tea.

# Crêpes Suzette with Warmed Peaches and Mangoes makes 6

50g plain flour
pinch of salt
2 eggs
150ml milk
10ml vegetable oil
butter for frying

for the sauce
50g butter
40g caster sugar
grated rind of ¹/₂ orange
juice of 1 orange
juice of ¹/₂ lemon
15ml Grand Marnier

to serve
400g tinned peaches, drained
1 large fresh mango, peeled, stoned and sliced
double cream
icing sugar
sprigs of mint

There is a great crêperie stand in Hampstead near where I live and they make the most amazing crêpes with all sorts of wonderful ingredients and toppings. They inspired me to make my own and this is my favourite fruity crêpes recipe. Of course, it would be just as good if you substituted melted chocolate for the double cream.

**Preparation time: 35 minutes**      **Cooking time: 20 minutes**

**1.** Sift the flour and salt in a bowl. Make a well in the centre and add the eggs then the milk and oil. Beat well and then let the batter stand for 30 minutes.

**2.** Heat a pan over high heat, add a knob of butter, ladle a portion of the batter in the pan and swirl around. Lift one side of the crêpe and if it is golden brown then flip it over to brown on the other side. Place on a plate and cover with foil and keep warm in the oven while you make the rest.

**3.** To make the sauce, heat a very large flat pan over high heat, melt the butter and add the sugar, orange rind and juice and lemon juice and stir well. Increase the heat and bring the sauce to simmering point and add the liqueur.

**4.** Fold the pancakes in half and then half again and place some peach and mango slices between each pancake. Gently place them in the pan to soak up all the juices of the sauce and warm through.

**5.** Carefully remove the crêpes and place them on a serving plate, ladling some of the sauce over the top. Serve with double cream, sprinkled with icing sugar and decorated with a mint sprig.

# Apple, Lychee and Blackberry Crumble serves 4

30g unsalted butter
3 large dessert apples, peeled and cored, diced
150g caster sugar
1/2 teaspoon ground cinnamon
80g fresh or tinned lychees, drained
150g blackberries
80g unsalted butter
100g plain flour
80g caster sugar

to serve
icing sugar
sprig of mint
ready-made custard

Almost everyone I know has had bad experiences with school dinners but I was fortunate at my school: the dinner ladies did a great job. When I first came to the UK my encounters with English food were at school – dishes such as fish and chips, shepherd's pie, cottage pie, Yorkshire puddings and apple crumble and custard – and I loved it. This is my take on English crumble, the Chinese influence here being lychees. I think the trio of apple, lychee and blackberry makes for a delicious combination. Great served with custard or a scoop of homemade lychee and vanilla ice cream.

Preparation time: 10 minutes          Cooking time: **35 minutes**

1. Preheat the oven to 180°C/350°F/Gas Mark 4.
2. Heat a wok or pan over high heat and melt the butter and sauté the apples. Add the caster sugar and the cinnamon and fry until the apples are crisp. Add the lychees and blackberries, stirring carefully. Remove from the heat and spoon the fruits into a gratin dish or small baking tray.
3. Rub together the butter, flour and caster sugar until crumbly. Sprinkle generously over the fruits to cover them. Bake for 20–25 minutes until golden brown.
4. Sprinkle with icing sugar, decorate with a sprig of mint and serve with Lychee and Vanilla Ice Cream (see page 37) or custard.

# 4. East Meets East

The Far East is an epicentre of glorious cuisine, from Chinese, Thai and Japanese to Vietnamese, Korean and Malay. It is known for an abundance of exotic ingredients and cooking styles. Even local traditions of eating can be found within each cuisine, such as dim sum in Chinese cooking and the special Nyonya food in Malaysia that fuses Chinese and Malay with a hint of Indonesian and Thai influence too.

And this is not 'new' news, people seem to have forgotten that the fusion of Chinese cooking with the rest of Asia has existed for many centuries. Many make a distinction between Chinese cooking and the rest of Asia but there are clear similarities, for example, the use of soy in Japan and China, while noodles feature throughout most of Asia, including Myanmar (Burma), Japan, Thailand and Vietnam (noodles originated in China). Even cooking techniques, such as stir frying, are common to many of these lands.

I want to celebrate the exchange of culinary knowledge between China and its neighbours – hence the theme East meets East – and long may it continue, for there is still much to be learned and discovered. We must give credit to all who try to introduce us to varied and diverse tastes and combinations rather than err on the safe side. I jumped for joy on a recent visit to a Chinese restaurant to find it served Thai fishcakes on a bed of crispy mung bean noodles! You'll find my version of Thai Salmon Fishcakes in this chapter, along with some of my favourite recipes from the Orient, including Thai Beef Salad, Beef Teriyaki Steak with Glutinous Rice, Peking Duck Nigiri Sushi and Black Bean Mussels in Japanese Beer. I hope you enjoy my fusion of Asian food or what I like to call 'Fusian' cuisine.

# Japanese Tofu in Chinese Sesame Soy Dipping Sauce   serves 2/makes 8

250g firm silken tofu, cut into 2cm squares
glutinous rice flour for dusting
250ml groundnut oil
1 sheet nori, finely shredded

for the dipping sauce
8 tablespoons light soy sauce
4 tablespoons mirin
1 tablespoon toasted black and white
 sesame seeds
1 teaspoon sugar
1 small red chilli, deseeded and finely chopped

This is similar to a Japanese dish called Agedashi Tofu (beancurd is tofu in Japanese, dofu in Mandarin Chinese). It is usually served in Japanese restaurants with a dashi broth (made with dried bonito fish flakes and konbu, a variety of kelp). My version has a different dip using light soy sauce, mirin (Japanese sweet rice wine), toasted sesame seeds, chillies and a sprinkle of sugar. This makes a simple but elegant starter. The Chinese ingredient here is glutinous rice flour, used to give a crunchy brown coating to the tofu. Try to buy fresh tofu, available from Chinese supermarkets, as nothing beats fresh.

Preparation time: 5 minutes          Cooking time: **8 minutes**

**1.** Dip the tofu cubes into the rice flour making sure each one is well coated.
**2.** Heat a wok over high heat and add the oil. Shallow fry the tofu, in batches if necessary, turning them over carefully to ensure they are golden on all sides. Drain the excess oil on kitchen paper.
**3.** Mix together the sauce ingredients.
**4.** Place the fried tofu on a serving plate, sprinkle with nori pieces and serve with the sesame dipping sauce.

# Prawn and Mung Bean Noodle Tempura   serves 2

1 egg yolk
200ml ice cold water
100g plain flour
8 raw tiger prawns, shelled and deveined
200g dried mung bean noodles, chopped into
 2–3cm lengths
350ml groundnut oil

Sweet Chilli Jam (see page 142)

Prawn tempura is a popular Japanese recipe usually made with Panko breadcrumbs, but I think Chinese mung bean noodles make for a delicious change because when fried they expand and become crispy. These tasty morsels make sophisticated starters dipped in sweet chilli jam.

Preparation time: **10 minutes**          Cooking time: **5 minutes**

**1.** Put the egg yolk in a bowl. Add the ice cold water and plain flour and mix together to make a batter.
**2.** Dip the prawns first in the batter and then into the chopped dry noodles so that they are well coated.
**3.** Heat a wok over high heat and add the groundnut oil. Deep-fry the tempura until the prawns turn pink and the coating is golden brown. Drain any excess oil on kitchen paper and serve immediately with Sweet Chilli Jam.

# Thai Salmon Fishcakes with Chinese Black Rice Vinegar Dip

**serves 4/makes 8**

for the fishcakes
*500g salmon fillet, roughly chopped*
*1 teaspoon Thai green curry paste*
   *(see page 131)*
*1 egg, beaten*
*2 tablespoons nam pla (fish sauce)*
*1 tablespoon caster sugar*
*2 tablespoons cornflour*
*juice of 1 lime*
*3 tablespoons freshly chopped coriander*
*pinch of salt and freshly ground black pepper*

*4–6 tablespoons groundnut oil*

for the dipping sauce
*6 tablespoons light soy sauce*
*2 tablespoons Chinese black rice vinegar*
*1 tablespoon ginger, grated*
*1 red chilli, deseeded and finely chopped*
*2 tablespoons freshly chopped coriander*

This recipe is one of my all-time favourites. The Thai green curry paste gives the fishcakes an incredible flavour and leaves you wanting more. You can make your own Thai green curry paste (see page 131), otherwise Oriental supermarkets usually stock dried pastes that are free from artificial additives and preservatives (which does save you from having to buy all the ingredients). Two of my favourite dips to go with this are shop bought sweet chilli sauce and Chinese black rice vinegar dip. I find the sharpness of the black rice vinegar complements the spicy fishcakes perfectly.

**Preparation time: 15 minutes**     **Cooking time: 8 minutes**

**1.** Combine all the ingredients for the fishcakes in a bowl.
**2.** Heat a wok over high heat and add the groundnut oil.
**3.** Drop tablespoons of the mixture into the wok and fry the mixture for 2–3 minutes until golden brown. Work in batches, adding more oil if necessary, then drain any excess oil on kitchen paper.
**4.** Mix together all the dipping sauce ingredients into a bowl and serve with the fishcakes.

# Vietnamese Rice Rolls with Chinese Peanut Chilli Beef

serves 4–6/makes 12

350g minced beef

for the beef marinade
½ teaspoon Chinese five-spice powder
1 tablespoon shaosing rice wine or dry sherry
1 teaspoon fish sauce (nam pla)
1 tablespoon cornflour

for the filling
1 tablespoon groundnut oil
2 garlic cloves, crushed and finely chopped
1 tablespoon freshly grated ginger
1 medium chilli, deseeded and chopped
50g diced courgettes
50g diced carrots
3 tablespoons fish sauce (nam pla)

12 rice paper rolls, presoaked in warm water
    for 10 minutes
50g crushed roasted peanuts

I usually make a peanut chilli beef stir fry using strips of sirloin steak. However, I discovered that by substituting mince, I had a divine filling for Vietnamese rice rolls. Vietnamese rice paper comes in a solid pack of translucent, wafer-thin sheets. They are hard to the touch and look brittle but are actually quite strong. After soaking just to soften them they make a delicious wrap for savoury fillings and a nice healthy change from fried spring rolls. This is a great starter to have at the centre of the table and for everyone to get involved and roll their own.

Preparation time: **10 minutes plus marinating**          Cooking time: **8 minutes**

**1.** Marinate the beef with the five-spice powder, rice wine and fish sauce for as long as possible. Just before cooking, add the cornflour and mix well.

**2.** Heat a wok over high heat and add the oil. Stir fry the garlic, ginger and chilli for less than 1 minute. Add the beef and stir fry for 1 minute until the meat starts to turn brown. Add the courgettes and carrots and stir fry for 2 minutes until the vegetables start to soften. Season with fish sauce.

**3.** To serve, place a softened rice paper on a plate, spoon a few tablespoons of the meat filling onto the rice paper, sprinkle with crushed roasted peanuts and roll up.

# Thai Beef Salad with a Chinese Twist   serves 1

1 tablespoon groundnut oil
1 x 250g sirloin steak
1 teaspoon Chinese five-spice powder
1 tablespoon shaosing rice wine or dry sherry
pinch of salt and freshly ground black pepper

1 spring onion, finely sliced
40g cucumber, sliced with a peeler into long strips
1 lemongrass stalk, finely sliced
1 red onion, finely sliced
2 red chillies, deseeded and chopped
1 tablespoon fish sauce (nam pla)
1 teaspoon brown sugar
2 tablespoons lime juice
handful of mint leaves, stripped from stems and
    roughly chopped
pinch of salt and freshly ground black pepper

handful of coriander
150g watercress

This can be made in advance and doubles as an easy sophisticated starter or a meal for one! Just increase the amount of ingredients required in the recipe for more servings. The Chinese twist to this recipe is the five-spice powder, which gives added flavour and fragrance to the beef while the shaosing rice wine provides sweetness to the meat. This subtle yet noticeably tastier difference makes this a winner at my dinner parties.

Preparation time: **10 minutes**          Cooking time: **10 minutes**

**1.** Heat the oil in a frying pan and fry the steak to taste. Season with five-spice powder, pour over the rice wine and sprinkle with salt and pepper. Set aside to cool slightly and then slice into strips.
**2.** Put the beef, and any cooking juices from the pan, in a bowl with the salad ingredients and mix well. Season with salt and pepper.
**3.** To serve, layer fresh coriander and fresh watercress leaves on a plate, top with the beef and salad mix and spoon some of the juices from the bottom of the bowl over the top.

# Miso Beef Saucy Stir Fry

**serves 4 as a starter or as a shared main**

2 tablespoons groundnut oil
500g beef fillet or rump steak, cut into strips
    4 x 2cm
1 tablespoon grated ginger

for the sauce
$^1/_2$ teaspoon Chinese five-spice powder
1 tablespoon red miso paste
1 tablespoon sake
1 tablespoon mirin
2 tablespoons soy sauce
2 teaspoons sugar
2 teaspoons rice vinegar
150ml hot beef stock

2 spring onions, finely chopped

This is a lovely dish to serve as a starter or as one of several main courses. Stir-fried beef is added to a delicious sauce that fuses Chinese five-spice powder, Japanese miso paste, sake, mirin, soy sauce, rice vinegar, stock and sugar. The sauce is reduced in the wok to give the beef a glorious thick, sweet and savoury coating. The fusion of Chinese and Japanese ingredients and flavours marries well, and works not only with beef but chicken thighs or salmon fillets too.

**Preparation time: 5 minutes**　　　**Cooking time: 10 minutes**

**1.** Heat a wok over high heat and add 1 tablespoon of the oil. Throw in the beef strips and stir fry over high heat for 1–2 minutes until tender. Set aside.

**2.** Wipe out the wok with kitchen paper, reheat it and add the remaining oil.

**3.** Meanwhile, put all the sauce ingredients in a bowl and stir well.

**4.** Add the ginger to the wok and stir fry for a few seconds, then add the sauce ingredients and bring to a simmer. Cook for about 3–4 minutes until it starts to thicken. Add the beef back in at the end and allow the sauce to reduce to a thick sticky texture, cooking for about 2–3 minutes.

**5.** Just before serving, throw in the spring onions, stir well and serve immediately with Green Salad (see page 147) for a starter or steamed rice for a main course.

# Peking Duck Nigiri Sushi   serves 4/makes 12

*1 large whole duck breast fillet, skin on*

*for the marinade*
*½ teaspoon Chinese five-spice powder*
*1 tablespoon sesame oil*
*3 tablespoons hoi sin sauce*
*3 tablespoons brown sugar*
*3 tablespoons water*
*1 tablespoon dark soy sauce*

*for the sushi rice*
*150g shortgrain sushi rice, washed until water runs clear*
*240ml water*
*½ teaspoon salt*
*2 tablespoons mirin*
*1 teaspoon sugar*
*2 tablespoons rice vinegar*
*2 tablespoons hot water*

*12 fine slices cucumber*
*12 fine slices spring onion*

I fell in love with sushi when I was about 11 years old. My family was preparing to move from South Africa to England and we went back to Taiwan to visit relatives before the relocation. It was at a sushi restaurant in Taipei near where my aunt lived that I first tried Sashimi (slices of raw fish) dipped in wasabi (blow-your-socks-off horseradish paste) and light soy. I remember my father telling me that I should hold my breath when eating this way, to avoid breathing in the wasabi which gives a burning pain between the eyes. It was quite a mind-blowing sensation – literally.

I didn't realise at the time but the Taiwanese are mad about Japanese food. My great-grandparents could speak Mandarin (the national Chinese language), Taiwanese dialect and Japanese. This influence came about because Japan occupied Taiwan for 50 years up until 1945. I'm not sure that the occupation was an entirely happy one but I'm happy to see a fusion of the two cuisines.

**Preparation time: 15 minutes plus marinating**          **Cooking time: 30 minutes**

**1.** Mix all the marinade ingredients in a bowl. Place the duck breast in a ziplock bag, pour over the marinade and leave to marinate for as long as possible, ideally overnight.

**2.** Drain the marinade off the duck into a small pan and bring to the boil. This makes a fantastic dipping sauce.

**3.** Preheat the oven to 220°C/425°F/Gas Mark 7. Place the duck breast, skin side down, in a wok or pan (no oil), and cook for about 1 minute until golden brown then turn over and do the same to the underside. Place on a roasting tray and cook for 15 minutes (the time can vary, depending on the size of the fillet and how rare you prefer your meat). At this temperature, it will be well done.

**4.** Meanwhile, put the rice and measured water in a medium pan with a tight-fitting lid. Boil the rice until only a little of the water covers the rice. Reduce the heat and leave the rice to simmer for about 10 minutes until all the water is absorbed.

**5.** Remove the pan from the heat and let it stand for about 10 minutes. Mix the rest of the seasoning ingredients in a bowl, stir well, and pour into the rice mixing with a flat wooden spoon or spatula.

**6.** Take a tablespoon of the sushi rice and make a small oval mound. Place a cucumber slice cut into the same size that fits on the top of the rice mound. Make 12 mounds.

**7.** Remove the duck from the oven and let it stand for a few minutes. Then slice the breast horizontally in half to give two pieces of meat, one with skin, the other without. Then slice each half to give 12 equal pieces, 6 with the fatty skin, the other 6 will be lean pieces of meat. Pile the slices on top of the rice and cucumber and serve with the dipping sauce and slices of spring onion, sharing out the lean and fatty duck portions among your guests.

# Chilli Beancurd and Mixed Oriental Mushroom Stir Fry   serves 4

1 tablespoon groundnut oil

2 garlic cloves, crushed and finely chopped

1 tablespoon freshly grated ginger

1 medium red chilli, deseeded and chopped

100g oyster mushrooms, halved if large

100g enoki mushrooms, separated into small
   bunches

100g shiitake mushrooms, sliced

400g fresh tofu (beancurd), cut into 2cm cubes

50ml vegetable stock

1 tablespoon chilli bean sauce (do-ban jiang)

dash of light soy sauce

2 spring onions, sliced diagonally

handful of coriander leaves, finely chopped

The chilli bean sauce, do-ban jiang, is the star here. It delivers a fiery heat that is irresistible to chilli lovers. This Sichuan-inspired dish fuses three different types of delectable oriental mushrooms: oyster, enoki and shiitake. If you are not a beancurd fan, you can always add a Chinese vegetable such as gai lan (Chinese broccoli) or pak choy instead. If you like more sauce, add extra stock or, for a thicker sauce, add a little blended cornflour or let the sauce reduce slightly. However, I like it just the way it is.

Preparation time: **7 minutes**          Cooking time: **4 minutes**

**1.** Heat a wok over high heat and add the groundnut oil. Add the garlic, ginger and chillies and stir fry for a few seconds. Add the mushrooms and stir fry for less than 1 minute. Add the tofu and carefully stir well.

**2.** Pour in the vegetable stock then add the chilli bean sauce and light soy sauce and cook for less than 1 minute. Add the sliced spring onions and coriander and serve immediately.

# Vietnamese Stir-fried Prawns with Chinese Leaf and Egg-fried Rice

serves 2

1 tablespoon groundnut oil
1 garlic clove, crushed and finely chopped
1 tablespoon freshly grated ginger
1 medium red chilli, deseeded and finely chopped
16 raw tiger prawns (about 200g), shelled and
  deveined
100g Chinese leaf, cut into 4cm slices
3 tablespoons fish sauce (nuoc mam or nam pla)
1 tablespoon Chinese black rice vinegar
4 tablespoons hot water
1 teaspoon sugar
small handful Thai basil leaves

Egg-fried Rice (see page 142)

Nuoc mam or fish sauce is an essential ingredient in Vietnamese cooking. It is also widely used in the Philippines (known as patis) and in Thailand (nam pla). It is made from fermented salted fish or shrimps and is rich brown in colour with a pungent fishy aroma and an intense salty flavour. In these countries, fish sauce is used in the same way the Chinese use soy sauce. In addition to its role as a seasoning ingredient in stir-fries it can be used to dress salads and add flavour to marinades or dipping sauces. This recipe is a fusion Chinese–Vietnamese stir fry using quintessential Chinese ingredients such as garlic and ginger with succulent tiger prawns and crunchy Chinese leaf finished off with fish sauce and aromatic Chinese black rice vinegar for a subtle edge and – for a touch of fragrance – not the usual coriander but Thai basil. It is served with Chinese egg-fried rice and is ready in minutes!

Preparation time: **15 minutes**       Cooking time: **5 minutes**

**1.** Heat a wok over high heat and add the oil. Stir fry the garlic and ginger for less than 1 minute. Add the chilli and prawns and stir fry until the prawns start to turn pink. Add the Chinese leaf and stir fry for less than 1 minute.

**2.** Season with the fish sauce and black rice vinegar. Add the hot water and sugar and stir well.

**3.** Sprinkle with the Thai basil leaves, remove the wok from the heat and serve immediately with Egg-fried Rice (see page 142).

# Black Bean Mussels in Japanese Beer  serves 2

2 tablespoons olive oil

3 garlic cloves, crushed and finely chopped

1 tablespoon freshly grated ginger

1 red chilli, deseeded and chopped

2 tablespoons fermented, salted black beans,
    washed and crushed

1kg mussels, washed and debearded

500ml Japanese beer

3 tablespoons light soy sauce

3 spring onions, chopped

handful of coriander leaves, chopped

I usually simply wok fry black bean mussels. However, on an uneventful occasion, while cooking the dish in the usual way, I happened to be sipping a cool variety of super dry Japanese beer. It seemed like the perfect match. The rest is history... and bitter-sweetly good.

Preparation time: **5 minutes**        Cooking time: **5 minutes**

**1.** Heat the wok over high heat and add the oil. Add the garlic, ginger, chillies and black beans and stir fry for less than 1 minute. Add the mussels and stir fry for less than 1 minute. Add the Japanese beer and cook until the mussels open, stirring occasionally. (Discard any that do not open.) Season with light soy sauce.

**2.** Sprinkle in the spring onion and coriander and serve immediately – try with the Smoked Paprika Sweet Potato Chips on page 143.

# Spicy Monkfish in Banana Leaves with Coconut Shrimp Sauce

**serves 2**

350g monkfish fillet
pinch of salt and ground white pepper

2 large pieces of banana leaf
8 toothpicks

for the sauce
1 tablespoon groundnut oil
1 garlic clove, crushed and finely chopped
1 tablespoon peeled and grated galangal
1 medium red chilli, deseeded and finely chopped
2 shallots, finely chopped
200ml coconut milk
1 teaspoon shrimp paste
1 teaspoon turmeric
2 tablespoon fish sauce (nam pla)
2 teaspoons palm sugar
juice of 1 lime

My favourite way of cooking fish is to steam it. It is easy to cook and, most importantly, it's the best way to tell if the fish is fresh as there's no fishy aroma once cooked. Using the bamboo steamer retains the moisture of the fish but if you wrap the fish in fresh banana leaves first, I find the leaves keep the fish especially moist and add a slight fragrance. The blackish-brown shrimp paste used to create the delicious sauce is made from fermented ground shrimp. It is widely used in South-east Asia and is a great ingredient for curries or sauces.

**Preparation time: 10 minutes**   **Cooking time: 6 minutes**

1. Wash the monkfish and pat it dry with kitchen paper. Cut it into 2 fillets.
2. Place the fillets on the banana leaf. Season well with salt and pepper and wrap the leaf around the fillets, securing with toothpicks.
3. Place the parcels in a bamboo steamer and put the lid on top. Place the steamer in a wok with boiling water, making sure the base of the steamer is not immersed in water. Steam the fish for 5–6 minutes.
4. Heat another wok or pan over high heat and add the oil. Stir fry the garlic and galangal and red chilli for less than 30 seconds. Add the shallots and stir fry until coloured.
5. Add the coconut milk and the shrimp paste and stir well. Add the turmeric, season with fish sauce, then add the palm sugar and lime juice.
6. To serve, place the parcels on a large serving plate, unwrap and pour the delicious sauce over the fish. Serve immediately with steamed rice.

# Wok-fried Fish in Fish Sauce (Yu Siang Yu) serves 2

1 red mullet, cleaned, skin on
1 tablespoon freshly grated ginger
pinch of salt and ground white pepper

4 tablespoons groundnut oil
1 tablespoon shaosing rice wine or dry sherry
4 tablespoons fish sauce (nam pla) mixed with
    1 teaspoon sugar
2 medium red chillies, deseeded and chopped
2 spring onions, sliced at an angle

My grandmother used to wok fry fish and the kitchen was filled with mouth-watering aromas. She would often wok fry fresh fish just seasoned with salt and then add a few splashes of light soy sauce and spring onions. The trick is to get the skin really crispy. To do this, you need to use quite a lot of oil and resist the urge to turn the fish over too soon. If you do, the fish will break and it can turn into a big mess. This is an art I have now perfected after several attempts, and for my East meets East theme I have adapted my grandmother's recipe to include the use of pungent fish sauce instead of light soy, thus creating my 'fishy fragrant fish' or Yu Siang Yu!

Preparation time: **5 minutes**       Cooking time: **15 minutes**

1. Wash and dry the mullet. Cut some slits into the sides and season well with ginger, salt and pepper.
2. Heat a wok over high heat and add the groundnut oil. Fry the fish on one side for 6 minutes until browned and then turn it over and cook over medium heat for a further 6 minutes. The skin should be crispy.
3. Add the rice wine and fish sauce with sugar. Let the fish cook in the sauce until the flesh is flaky and tender. Add the chillies and spring onions to the wok.
4. Transfer to a serving plate and serve with Mushroom and Shrimp-fried Chinese leaf and Jasmine Rice (see pages 142 and 145).

# Prawn and Lemon Wasabi 'Liang Mein' (Cool Noodle) Salad  serves 4

100g soba (buckwheat) noodles
100g Japanese green tea noodles
dash of sesame oil
100g chopped carrots
4 spring onions, sliced lengthways
100g red pepper, sliced
100g yellow pepper, sliced
500g prepared tiger prawns (cooked and peeled)

for the dressing
100g olive oil
1 tablespoon light soy sauce
1 tablespoon rice vinegar
1/2 teaspoon wasabi paste
1 tablespoon lemon juice

to garnish
1 tablespoon toasted white sesame seeds
coriander leaves

'Liang Mein', Mandarin for 'cool noodle salad', is enjoyed all over the Far East from Japan, China, Thailand, Singapore, Malaysia, Burma, Laos, Indonesia, the Philippines and more. It can be eaten as a main course and is rather refreshing in hot summers. Liang Mein can have different toppings and ingredients ranging from meats to seafood medleys or be kept vegetarian. This recipe fuses Japanese soba (buckwheat) noodles and green tea noodles with a wasabi, lemon and light soy dressing and juicy tiger prawns, topped with a generous sprinkle of toasted sesame seeds.

**Preparation time: 15 minutes**        **Cooking time: 3 minutes**

1. Cook the noodles according to the instructions on the packets, then drain and refresh under cold running water. Drizzle with sesame oil, mix well to prevent them from sticking together and place in a large bowl.
2. Prepare the vegetables and distribute evenly over the noodles.
3. Put all the dressing ingredients in a bowl and mix well. Pour the dressing over the noodles, add the prawns and toss well.
4. Divide the noodles onto serving plates, sprinkle with toasted sesame seeds and coriander leaves and serve.

# Chicken Katsu Curry  serves 4

4 large skinless chicken breasts
200g plain flour
4 eggs, beaten
300g Panko breadcrumbs (use ordinary if Panko
    are not available)
500ml groundnut oil

for the katsu curry sauce (makes 1 litre)
2 tablespoons butter
2 garlic cloves, crushed and finely chopped
$^1/_2$ large onion, chopped
3 Granny Smith apples, chopped
300ml boiling water
2 bananas, sliced
2 tablespoons honey
1 tablespoon turmeric powder
$^1/_2$ teaspoon hot Madras curry powder
2 tablespoons ketchup
450ml chicken stock
500ml boiling water
2 teaspoons cornflour blended with a little of the
    measured water
1 tablespoon salt
1 tablespoon ground black pepper

This is a Japanese recipe (the word 'katsu' refers in Japanese to the fried chicken) which is also a popular favourite in Taiwan – so much so that there is an adapted Taiwanese version known as Pai-Gu Fan which uses pork chops on the bone and is similarly prepared but substitutes tapioca flour for Panko breadcrumbs. Both should be available in oriental supermarkets. The curry sauce to accompany the katsu is easy to make but if you are short of time, you can buy ready-made cubes that simply need making up with water. This is delicious with steamed rice or a serving of Chinese flat udon noodles.

Preparation time: **30 minutes**         Cooking time: **30 minutes**

**1.** First make the sauce. Heat a large pan over high heat and melt the butter. Sauté the garlic and onions then add apples, the boiling water, bananas, honey, turmeric, Madras powder and ketchup. Bring the sauce to the boil and add the chicken stock, water, blended cornflour, salt and pepper. Cook for 20 minutes, stirring occasionally.

**2.** Strain the sauce through a sieve into a bowl, discarding any solids. Cover with foil and keep warm in the oven (you can reheat it in a small pan to make sure it is piping hot before serving).

**3.** Make some slits in the chicken breasts to ensure that the heat will get through. Coat the breasts in plain flour and shake off any excess. Dip the breasts into the beaten egg, then coat evenly with the breadcrumbs.

**4.** Heat a wok over high heat and add the groundnut oil. Deep fry the chicken breasts for 5–6 minutes (depending on size) until golden brown. You may need to work in batches; keep them warm on a plate covered with foil in the oven until all the pieces are cooked.

**5.** Serve the chicken with the curry sauce, steamed rice or udon noodles and Chinese Pickled Salad (see page 146).

# Malaysian-style Satay Chicken
# with Coconut Peanut Sauce   serves 2

200g skinless chicken breast, sliced then cubed
    into bite-sized chunks
1 teaspoon ground cumin
1 teaspoon ground coriander
1 teaspoon ground lemongrass (found in
    oriental stores)
1 teaspoon ground white pepper
$1/2$ teaspoon turmeric
pinch of salt
1 tablespoon groundnut oil
100ml hot chicken stock
freshly chopped coriander

for the peanut sauce
1 tablespoon groundnut oil
1 garlic clove, crushed and finely chopped
1 tablespoon freshly grated ginger
1 medium red chilli, deseeded and chopped
1 large shallot, peeled and finely chopped
1 teaspoon ground cumin
1 teaspoon ground coriander
1 teaspoon ground lemongrass
5 tablespoons roasted peanuts, ground with a
    pestle and mortar or grinder
300ml fresh chicken stock
1 tablespoon smooth or crunchy peanut butter
1 tablespoon soft brown sugar
400ml coconut milk
salt and ground white pepper

This is my version of a Malaysian satay recipe. I infuse the satay sauce with coconut milk and serve it on a bed of egg noodles. This may seem like a time-consuming recipe but it's worth every effort. The result is a creamy, nutty and fiery chicken curry that will have your guests asking for seconds. Serve this curry with egg noodles or jasmine rice and wash it down with a bottle of Chinese beer.

Preparation time: **10 minutes**        Cooking time: **40 minutes**

1. Put the cubed chicken in a bowl and season with the salt and spices. Heat a wok over high heat and add the oil. Stir fry the chicken for about 6 minutes until golden brown. Stir in some of the chicken stock if the wok gets too hot or the chicken sticks to the sides of the wok and becomes too dry. Transfer the pieces to a plate, cover with foil and keep warm.

2. Rinse and clean the wok (I use a bamboo brush and water), reheat over high heat and add the groundnut oil. Stir fry the garlic and ginger for less than 1 minute. Add the chilli and shallot and stir fry for less than 1 minute. Add the cumin, coriander and lemongrass and stir fry for a few seconds. Add the crushed roasted peanuts and stir fry for less than 1 minute.

3. Add the chicken stock and bring to the boil. Stir in the peanut butter and brown sugar and season with salt and ground white pepper.

4. Blitz the sauce with a stick blender but don't blend until completely smooth, you want to keep the texture of the peanuts. Stir in the coconut milk, bring to a simmer, and add the chicken pieces.

5. Sprinkle with coriander and serve with Jasmine Rice (see page 142) or noodles.

# Oriental Pork Chops with Chinese Pickled Salad serves 2

2 x 230g pork loin
salt and freshly ground black pepper

for the marinade
2–3 large red chillies, deseeded and chopped
4 large garlic cloves, crushed and finely chopped
1 teaspoon freshly grated ginger
2 tablespoons fish sauce (nam pla)
1 teaspoon soft brown sugar
juice of 1 lime
2 tablespoons light soy sauce
2 tablespoons mirin
2 tablespoons groundnut oil
2 tablespoons chopped basil
2 tablespoons chopped coriander

Chinese Pickled Salad (see page 146)

This is a delicious recipe that fuses a few ingredients of the Orient: nam pla (pungent fish sauce used predominantly in Thai and Vietnamese cuisine), mirin (sweet Japanese rice wine) and light soy sauce (common to Chinese and Japanese cooking). The result is a subtle but wonderful happening of fishy, salty, sour, spicy, sweet flavours all at once. It reminds me of the delightful Sichuan-Chinese style of cooking that often fuses all these taste sensations. I hope this is one dish that will become a firm household favourite and, if you don't eat pork, use a firm-fleshed fish such as cod or halibut instead.

Preparation time: **10 minutes plus marinating**
Cooking time: **20–25 minutes**

1. Whizz together all the marinade ingredients in a blender. Season the pork loin with salt and pepper. Pour the marinade into a ziplock bag with the pork loins and marinate for as long as possible, ideally overnight.
2. Preheat the oven to 200°C/400°F/Gas Mark 6.
3. Place the pork in a roasting tin with a few spoonfuls of the marinade. Cook in the oven for 25 minutes.
4. Make the Pickled Salad (see page 146) and mix well to allow the sauce to pickle the vegetables.
5. Pour the remaining marinade into a small pan and heat.
6. To serve, invert a bowlful of steamed rice onto the centre of the plate, dress with pickle salad, place the pork loin on top and drizzle over the fragrant sauce.

# Beef Teriyaki Steak with Glutinous Rice  serves 2

2 x 180g sirloin steaks
4 tablespoons groundnut oil

for the marinade
2 garlic cloves, crushed and chopped
1 tablespoon freshly grated ginger
4 tablespoons sake
4 tablespoons mirin
100ml light soy sauce
freshly ground black pepper

350ml water
200g glutinous rice, washed until the water runs
    clear, then soaked in 1 litre water for
    20 minutes to soften

Fusing two great recipes: Japanese teriyaki-style beef and sticky rice. In Japanese 'teri' means 'shine' and 'yaki' means to grill, which is the usual way of cooking teriyaki, pieces of skewered marinated meat dipped in teriyaki sauce and then grilled. However, teriyaki sauce can also be used to flavour stir fries and in this case the sweet savoury sauce is cooked with juicy steaks. Intermittent mouthfuls of the two are divine.

Preparation time: **40 minutes plus marinating**
Cooking time: **25 minutes**

**1.** Combine all the marinade ingredients together. Put in a ziplock bag and marinate the steak in it for as long as possible, ideally overnight.

**2.** Bring the water to the boil in a large pan and add the glutinous rice. Cover and boil for 15 minutes. Remove the pan from the heat and let the rice cook in the steam for a further 10 minutes.

**3.** Heat a wok over high heat and add the groundnut oil. Remove the steak from the marinade and fry on one side for 2–3 minutes then turn it over. Pour in the marinade and cook the steak for a further 1 minute in the sauce until the sauce thickens (the steak will be medium). Season with extra ground black pepper.

**4.** Place the steak on a large serving plate. Press some sticky rice into a small bowl then invert it onto the plate next to the beef. Drizzle the remaining teriyaki sauce from the wok onto the beef. Serve immediately – this one is great with Soy and Sesame French Beans or with Chinese Pea Shoots in Sesame and Garlic (see pages 148 and 149).

# Thai Chicken Green Curry with Jasmine Rice  serves 4

for the curry

3 tablespoons groundnut oil

300g skinless chicken thighs

500ml coconut milk

3 tablespoons Thai green curry paste (see below)

90g bamboo shoots, sliced

50g baby corn, sliced

50g closed cup mushrooms

1/2 red pepper, sliced

50g beansprouts

4 tablespoons freshly chopped coriander

10 fresh Thai basil leaves

for the Thai green curry paste

5 garlic cloves, crushed and finely chopped

6 fresh green chillies, deseeded and finely chopped

2 fresh lemongrass stalks

3 tablespoons coriander roots, chopped

2cm fresh galangal or ginger

1 large shallot or red onion

1 teaspoon grated lime peel (preferably kaffir lime)

juice of 1 lime

2 teaspoons ground cumin

1 teaspoon coriander seeds

1 teaspoon black peppercorns

pinch of salt

Along with Thai red curry, this is one of my favourite Thai recipes of all and I thought I must include it. It's not difficult to make your own Thai green curry paste but you can buy the sauce too. I like to use chicken thighs instead of breast as I find them juicier, but use what you prefer. You can also use tiger prawns or a medley of vegetables. In fact there could be a Chinese twist to this recipe if you use dofu (fresh or fried beancurd or tofu) instead of meat or fish. The fried beancurd would act as a sponge for the delicious curry sauce... a splendid idea.

Preparation time: **15 minutes**     Cooking time: **15 minutes**

**1.** To make the Thai green curry paste, whizz all the ingredients in a blender. Transfer the sauce to a bowl (it will keep, covered, for up to 1 week in the fridge).

**2.** Heat a wok over high heat and add the groundnut oil. Stir fry the chicken thighs for 6–7 minutes until golden brown. Set aside.

**3.** Wipe out the wok with kitchen paper and reheat it. Add 250ml coconut milk and the Thai green curry paste to the wok and stir well. Add in the bamboo shoots, baby corn and mushrooms. Stir in the rest of the coconut milk and bring to the boil. Throw in the red pepper, beansprouts and the chicken thighs and stir well for 2 minutes.

**4.** Garnish with coriander and Thai basil leaves and serve with Jasmine Rice (see page 142).

# Burmese-style Beef Curry with Vermicelli Rice Noodles  *serves 2*

*2 tablespoons groundnut oil*
*2 shallots, peeled and chopped*
*1 tablespoon shrimp paste*
*350g sirloin steak, cubed*
*300ml coconut milk*
*1 lemongrass stalk, chopped*
*¹/₂ teaspoon soft brown sugar*
*1 tablespoon ground coriander seed*
*2 tablespoons fish sauce (nam pla)*

*for the paste*
*4 garlic cloves, crushed and finely chopped*
*1 tablespoon freshly grated ginger*
*2 red chillies, deseeded and chopped*
*1 large onion, peeled and chopped*
*1 teaspoon turmeric*

*1 handful chopped fresh coriander*
*1 handful chopped Thai basil leaves*

*160g vermicelli rice noodles*

A delicious Burmese curry that you can adapt to your taste. If you cannot take chillies, reduce the quantity I give or, if you love spiciness, increase the number of chillies and you can also add some crushed dried chillies. This recipe can be served with steamed rice but I love Chinese vermicelli rice noodles: they make for a lighter meal and marry well for our East meets East theme.

**Preparation time: 10 minutes**          **Cooking time: 15 minutes**

**1.** Blend all the paste ingredients together.
**2.** Heat a wok over high heat, add the oil and stir fry the shallots with the shrimp paste for less than 1 minute. Add the paste ingredients and stir fry for 1 minute. Add the steak and stir fry for 2 minutes until browned on all sides.
**3.** Stir in the coconut milk. (For a thinner sauce, you could also add a little chicken stock at this stage. For a creamier curry, you could add some coconut cream.) Add the lemongrass, the brown sugar, ground coriander and fish sauce. Bring to the boil and sprinkle with a handful of chopped fresh coriander and Thai basil leaves.
**4.** Bring a large pan of water to the boil and cook the vermicelli rice noodles according to the packet instructions, drain and place in 2 serving bowls. Ladle curry over the noodles and serve immediately.

# Chicken Yakitori Sticks with Sesame Steamed Vinegar Rice and Chinese Pickled Salad serves 4

400g skinless chicken breast, thickly sliced

for the marinade
120ml light soy sauce
120ml sake
120ml mirin
2 tablespoons caster sugar

for the vinegar rice
250g sushi-style short grain rice, washed until
    the water runs clear and drained well
500ml water
2 tablespoons rice vinegar
toasted white and black sesame seeds

8–10 bamboo skewers, soaked in water

Chinese Pickled Salad (see page 146)

This is one of my favourite Japanese recipes and, teamed with Chinese pickled salad and sushi-style vinegar rice, it makes a healthy dinner that is easy to cook. You could also make the chicken sticks as a starter accompanied with the pickled salad. 'Yakitori' simply means grilled skewered meat. This recipe sees the liberal use of soy sauce – the one ingredient that Chinese and Japanese cuisines have in common. Wonderful!

Preparation time: **20 minutes plus marinating**          Cooking time: **15 minutes**

**1.** Put all the marinade ingredients into a bowl and mix well. Add the chicken to the bowl and marinate for as long as possible, ideally overnight.

**2.** Preheat the oven to 180°C/350°F/Gas Mark 4 or heat a griddle pan until hot.

**3.** Skewer the chicken breasts then bake in the oven for 15 minutes or on a hot griddle, turning regularly, until brown on all sides.

**4.** Put the rice and water in a medium pan with a tight-fitting lid and boil until only a little of the water covers the rice. Reduce the heat and let the rice simmer for about 10 minutes until all the water is absorbed. Remove the pan from the heat and let it stand for a few minutes, then add the rice vinegar and mix well with a flat wooden spoon or spatula.

**5.** Make the Pickled Salad (see page 146) and mix well to allow the sauce to pickle the vegetables.

**6.** Put the Chinese Pickled Salad on a plate and top with the chicken yakitori sticks. Serve the steamed vinegar rice, sprinkled with sesame seeds, in a separate bowl.

# Mini Chocolate Puddings with Fresh Lychees and Melted Chocolate serves 4

85g soft margarine
100g self-raising flour
80g caster sugar
2 eggs
25g cocoa powder
25g plain chocolate (70% cocoa solids), broken into squares
100g milk chocolate, broken into squares
200g fresh lychees

The East meets East influence in this recipe is the liberal use of fresh lychees and the reliable bamboo steamer to ensure the chocolate puddings are cooked to perfection. Oh, and don't forget the melted chocolate: this will have your guests begging for more.

Preparation time: **20 minutes**          Cooking time: **45 minutes**

1. Grease 4 individual metal pudding basins or ramekin dishes.
2. Put the margarine, flour, sugar, eggs and cocoa powder into a mixing bowl and beat until the mixture is smooth and combined. Chop the chocolate pieces and add them to the mixture.
3. Spoon the mixture into the pudding basins and smooth over the tops – they should be about half full. Cover each one with some parchment paper or baking paper and then cover with a piece of pleated foil.
4. Place the puddings in a large bamboo steamer over a pan or wok with boiling water. Make sure the base is not immersed in water. Cook for 40 minutes until the puddings have risen and are light and springy to touch. Remove from the heat and keep warm in the steamer.
5. Put the milk chocolate pieces into a heatproof bowl. Place it over a pan of boiling water and melt the chocolate.
6. Run a knife round the edges of the pudding basins and carefully invert the chocolate puddings onto serving plates. Decorate with fresh lychees on the side, pour over the melted chocolate and serve immediately.

# Chocolate Coconut Ice Cream    serves 4

2 eggs plus 2 egg yolks
115g caster sugar
300ml single cream
115g plain chocolate (70% cocoa solids),
    broken into squares
115g coconut cream
300ml double cream
3 tablespoons Jamaica rum

to serve
icing sugar
dried strawberry pieces

This is not quite an East meets East dessert but I just had to sneak it into the book because it's one of my favourites. This is really satisfying with a hint of Jamaica rum (so perhaps it's a case of East Indies meet West Indies?) topped off with pieces of dried strawberry. It makes a great finale to a meal.

Preparation time: **10 minutes**          Cooking time: **5 minutes**
Freezing time: **between 25 minutes and 5 hours depending on method**

**1.** Put the eggs, yolks and caster sugar into a heatproof bowl and beat until blended.
**2.** Put the single cream, chocolate and coconut cream in a small pan over medium heat until the chocolate melts.
**3.** Pour the coconut and chocolate mixture onto the egg mixture and set the bowl over a pan of boiling water. Heat for 2 minutes and gently stir the mixture then remove from the heat and allow to cool.
**4.** Fold the double cream and rum into the cooled mixture. It is then ready to pour into an ice-cream machine. Follow the manufacturer's instructions to churn the mixture. If you don't have a machine, transfer the mixture to a freezerproof bowl, cover and freeze for 2–3 hours until just frozen. Then, using a fork or whisk, break up any ice crystals. Return it to the freezer for a further 2 hours, remove and break up the ice again, then freeze until solid. Just before serving, transfer it to the fridge to allow it to soften a little.
**5.** Serve with a little icing sugar and a few pieces of dried strawberry.

# Coconut Bananas in Maple Syrup and Toasted Sesame Seeds serves 4

*400ml coconut milk*
*2 tablespoons soft brown sugar*
*pinch of salt*
*4 underripe bananas, peeled and sliced into 2cm thick slices*
*4 tablespoons toasted white sesame seeds*
*100ml maple syrup*

Sesame is available in various forms: pastes, oils and seeds. The seeds are a popular ingredient in the cuisines of Japan, China and Korea. Dry-toasting enhances their flavour, adds a little crunch and colours them an inviting golden-brown. This is an easy dessert – the bananas are cooked in coconut milk and served with a generous sprinkle of toasted sesame seeds and a drizzle of maple syrup. A bed of vanilla ice cream can be added especially for ice-cream lovers.

Preparation: **10 minutes**          Cooking time: **10 minutes**

1. Heat the wok over medium heat, add the coconut milk, sugar and salt and stir until the sugar has dissolved. Add the banana slices and cook until soft and warmed.
2. Serve immediately, scattered with toasted sesame seeds and drizzled with maple syrup.

# Fresh Mango and Vanilla Coconut Sticky Rice    serves 4

600ml coconut milk
200g glutinous rice, washed, soaked in water for
    30 minutes to soften and then drained well
1 vanilla pod
4 tablespoons soft brown sugar
pinch of salt
2 large ripe mangoes, peeled, stoned and sliced

sprig of mint

This is one of those recipes where it's easy to see the marriage of Far Eastern ingredients. This is a well-known Thai dessert which can be found in most Thai restaurants. Yet it can also be found on street-hawker stands in Malaysia and Singapore and in restaurants in Taiwan. This dessert uses mangoes (which originated in India but have since made their way all over the Far East) and coconut milk, which is widely used in savoury and sweet dishes in Thailand, Vietnam, Indonesia and Malaysia. However, what fuses the two ingredients together, aptly enough, is the sticky glutinous rice, a feature of both Thai and Chinese desserts. The rice is also cooked in true Chinese style – in a bamboo steamer! For an added little twist, a vanilla pod contributes its delightful fragrance to the dish.

Preparation time: **30 minutes**        Cooking time: **20 minutes**

**1.** Pour 400ml of the coconut milk into a large pan. Add the rice, vanilla pod, 2 tablespoons of the sugar and the salt. Stir and bring to the boil. Cook until all the coconut milk has been absorbed into the rice.

**2.** Transfer the rice onto a heatproof plate and put it in a bamboo steamer over a wok or pan of boiling water. Make sure the base of the steamer is not immersed in water. Steam the rice for 15 minutes until soft and sticky. Turn off the heat and leave the rice covered in the steamer to keep warm.

**3.** Heat the rest of the coconut milk in a small pan with the remaining soft brown sugar and stir until the sugar has dissolved.

**4.** Spoon the sticky rice into a bowl and invert it onto a plate. Make 4 servings in this way. Top with fresh mango slices, pour over some sweetened coconut milk and decorate with a sprig of mint.

# 5. Rice and Other Side Dishes

From Jasmine Rice to Coriander Couscous, the sides are a simple selection of recipes that are designed to complement the main 'stars' on any occasion – whether preparing a family meal or dishing up in front of guests.

    With a few exceptions, these accompaniments are mostly vegetarian and I have created them with ease of preparation in mind while ensuring they deliver maximum flavour. My selection also continues the themes of my four main chapters, from Modern Takeaway Favourites such as the familiar Egg-fried Rice to a simple family favourite, Chinese Pea Shoots in Sesame and Garlic, to reflect the traditional home cooking celebrated in Chapter 2. The fusion of East and West is picked up in the recipe for Soy and Sesame French Beans and, finally, the East on East influence is understated but discernable in the Chinese Pickled Salad recipe – my take on Korean-style *kimchi* (otherwise known as fiery pickled Chinese leaf salad). Enjoy!

# Jasmine Rice serves 4

350g jasmine rice, washed until the water
  runs clear
600ml boiled water

**Preparation time: 2 minutes**          **Cooking time: 20 minutes**

**1.** Place the rice in a heavy-based saucepan and add the boiled water. Bring to the boil then cover with a tight-fitting lid and reduce to a low heat. Cook for 15–20 minutes. Uncover the pan and remove from the heat. Fluff up the rice grains with a fork and serve immediately.

# Egg-fried Rice serves 4

2 tablespoons groundnut oil
2 eggs, beaten
30g Char Siu Pork (see page 30), diced
50g cooked baby shrimps
50g frozen peas
400g cooked cold jasmine rice (see above)
2 tablespoons light soy sauce
1 tablespoon sesame oil
2 pinches ground white pepper

**Preparation time: 7 minutes**          **Cooking time: 5 minutes**

**1.** Heat a wok over high heat and add the groundnut oil. Scramble the beaten eggs and set aside on a plate.

**2.** Into the same wok, throw in the Char Siu Pork, shrimps and frozen peas and stir fry for less than 1 minute. Add the rice and mix well until the rice has broken down.

**3.** Add the egg back into the wok and season with light soy sauce, sesame oil and a pinch of ground white pepper and serve immediately.

# Sweet Chilli Jam serves 2

100ml water
5 tablespoons granulated sugar
2 medium red chillies, chopped

**Preparation time: 2 minutes**          **Cooking time: 5 minutes**

**1.** Boil the water in a pan, add the sugar and stir to dissolve. Add the chillies and boil in the liquid for about 5 minutes. Pour into a blender and blitz. Transfer to a dipping bowl and set aside. The sauce will thicken and become jammy once cooled.

# Smoked Paprika Sweet Potato Chips serves 4

3 tablespoons olive oil
1 teaspoon salt
1 teaspoon smoked paprika
freshly ground black pepper
700g sweet potatoes, peeled and cut into chips

**Preparation time: 7 minutes**     **Cooking time: 30 minutes**

**1.** Preheat the oven to 180°C/350°F/Gas Mark 4.
**2.** Put the oil, salt, paprika and black pepper in a roasting tin, add the sweet potato and toss
well to coat in the seasoned oil. Roast for 30 minutes and serve immediately.

# Steamed Gai Lan (Chinese Broccoli)
# with Garlic Oyster Sauce   serves 4

340g gai lan (Chinese broccoli), washed, tough
    stems peeled, and then cut diagonally into
    5cm lengths
1 tablespoon groundnut oil
1 tablespoon freshly grated garlic
1 tablespoon freshly grated ginger
2 tablespoons oyster sauce
1 tablespoon sesame oil

**Preparation time: 2 minutes**          **Cooking time: 6 minutes**

**1.** Bring 1 litre water to the boil in a wok. Put the gai lan on a heatproof plate, transfer to a bamboo steamer, put the lid on and place it over the wok. Make sure the base of the steamer is not immersed in the water and steam for 2 minutes. Turn off the heat and keep the gai lan warm in the steamer.

**2.** Heat another wok or a pan and add the groundnut oil. Stir fry the garlic and ginger for less than 1 minute and add the oyster sauce and sesame oil, stir well, take off the heat and drizzle over the steamed gai lan.

# Mushroom and Shrimp Fried Chinese Leaf serves 4

1 tablespoon vegetable oil
1 garlic clove, crushed and finely chopped
1 red chilli, deseeded and finely chopped
2 dried Chinese mushrooms, soaked in hot
   water for 20 minutes, stems discarded
40g dried shrimps, soaked in hot water for
   20 minutes
350g Chinese leaf, cut into 2cm slices
1 tablespoon light soy sauce
1 tablespoon rice vinegar
1 teaspoon caster sugar
dash of sesame oil

**Preparation time: 25 minutes**       **Cooking time: 4 minutes**

**1.** Heat a wok over high heat, add the oil and stir fry the garlic and chilli for less than
1 minute, then add the Chinese mushrooms and shrimps and stir fry for less than
1 minute. Add the Chinese leaf and stir fry for 2 minutes until wilted slightly. Stir in
the light soy sauce, rice vinegar and caster sugar. Add a dash of sesame oil and serve
immediately.

# Dried Scallops and Shrimp Celery Stir Fry serves 4

1 tablespoon vegetable oil
1 tablespoon shrimp paste
1 garlic clove, crushed and finely chopped
1 red chilli, deseeded and chopped
40g dried shrimps, soaked in hot water for
   20 minutes
2 dried scallops, soaked in hot water for
   20 minutes, finely chopped
6 celery stalks, cut into thin slices
1 tablespoon oyster sauce
1 teaspoon sugar

**Preparation time: 25 minutes**       **Cooking time: 4–5 minutes**

**1.** Heat a wok over high heat, add the vegetable oil and stir in the shrimp paste. Add the
garlic and chilli and stir fry for less than 1 minute. Add the dried shrimps and dried
scallops and stir fry for less than 1 minute. Add the celery stalks and stir fry for about
2 minutes. Stir in the oyster sauce and sugar and serve immediately.

# Steamed Pak Choy or Broccoli serves 4

1 litre water
340g pak choy or broccoli

**Preparation time: 2 minutes**     **Cooking time: 2–3 minutes**

**1.** Bring 1 litre water to the boil in a wok. Put the pak choy on a heatproof plate, transfer to a bamboo steamer, put the lid on and place it over the wok, ensuring the base of the steamer is not submerged in the water, and steam for 2 minutes. Turn off the heat and keep the pak choy warm in the steamer until ready to serve.


# Chinese Pickled Salad serves 4

$^{1}/_{2}$ cucumber
2 small carrots
$^{1}/_{2}$ Chinese leaf

for the dressing
1 red chilli, deseeded and finely chopped
1 tablespoon mirin
1 tablespoon light soy sauce
$^{1}/_{2}$ tablespoon caster sugar

**Preparation time: 7 minutes**

**1.** Combine all the dressing ingredients in a bowl and mix well.
**2.** Slice the cucumber and carrots into thin slices using a vegetable peeler. Slice the Chinese leaf into 1cm slices.
**3.** Add the dressing to the vegetables and let the dressing pickle the salad. Cover the bowl with clingfilm and refrigerate.

# Green Salad and Oriental Dressing  serves 4

50g mizuna leaf
50g rocket
50g Chinese leaf, shredded
$^1/_2$ red onion, sliced
2 salad tomatoes, sliced
4 yellow cherry tomatoes, halved
2 large handfuls coriander, finely chopped

for the dressing
2 tablespoon olive oil
4 tablespoons lemon juice
1 tablespoon light soy sauce
$^1/_2$ teaspoon freshly grated garlic
$^1/_2$ teaspoon freshly grated ginger
1 teaspoon rice vinegar
pinch of sea salt and freshly ground black pepper

**Preparation time: 5 minutes**

**1.** Combine all the dressing ingredients and mix well.
**2.** Put all the salad ingredients in a bowl, pour the dressing over, toss well and serve.

# Soy and Sesame French Beans  serves 4

1 tablespoon vegetable oil

1 garlic clove, crushed and finely chopped

300g French beans, trimmed, washed
  and dried

1 tablespoon light soy sauce

dash of sesame oil

1 teaspoon toasted white sesame seeds

1 teaspoon toasted black sesame seeds

**Preparation time: 1 minute**          **Cooking time: 3 minutes**

**1.** Heat a wok over high heat and add the oil. Stir fry the garlic and for less than 1 minute, add the French beans and stir fry for a further minute. Season with light soy sauce and sesame oil and stir well.

**2.** Transfer to a serving plate, sprinkle with sesame seeds and serve immediately.

# Chinese Pea Shoots in Sesame and Garlic  serves 4

1 teaspoon groundnut oil
1 garlic clove, crushed and finely chopped
300g pea shoots, trimmed, washed well and dried
   (or use spinach)
1 teaspoon sesame oil
pinch of salt

**Preparation time: 1 minute**          **Cooking time: 1 minute**

**1.** Heat a wok over high heat, add the oil. Stir fry the garlic for less than 1 minute, add the pea shoots and stir fry until slightly wilted. Add the sesame oil and salt and serve immediately.

# Coriander Couscous  serves 4

350ml chicken or vegetable stock
250g couscous
salt and freshly ground black pepper
fresh coriander leaves, finely chopped

**Preparation time: 2 minutes**          **Cooking time: 5 minutes**

**1.** Heat the stock in a pan. Add the couscous and stir well. Allow the couscous to absorb all the stock and season with salt and freshly ground black pepper. Toss the coriander through the couscous and serve.

# Ching's Menu Planner

## For a buffet party for 8

### Starters
Peking Duck (p.14)
Sesame Prawn Toast (p.15)
Steamed Pork and Prawn Sui Mai
    Dumplings (p.19)
Sweet and Sour Chicken Sticks (p.12)

### Mains
Sichuan Pepper Prawns (p.25)
Bacon and Egg-fried Rice (p.28)
Kung Po Chicken (p.32)
Chilli and Pepper Squid (p.25)

### Dessert
Lychee and Vanilla Ice Cream (p.37)

## For a Chinese picnic

Char Siu Pork (p.30)
Guangdong Duck with Mango
    Salsa (p.84)
Vegetable Bao (p.48)
Nutty Chicken Cool Noodle
    Salad (p.29)
Eastern-style Tuna Salade
    Niçoise (p.89)
Green Salad and Oriental
    Dressing (p.147)
Spring Onion Flatbread (p.33)
Scones with Blueberry and Lychee
    Compôte (p.104)
Mango Pudding (p.36)

## For a first date

### Starter
Japanese Tofu in Chinese Sesame Soy
    Dipping Sauce (p.110)

### Main
Black Bean Mussels in Japanese
    Beer (p.120)

### Dessert
Fresh Mango and Vanilla Coconut
    Sticky Rice (p.139)

# For children

## Starters
Ketchup Prawns (p.78)
Green Salad and Oriental
    Dressing (p.147)

## Main
Oriental-style Meatballs and Spicy
    Coconut Noodles (p.97)

## Dessert
Lychee and Mango Trifle (p.104)

# For Chinese guests

## Starters
Steamed Egg with Scallops, Chinese
    Mushroom and Caviar (p.43)
Peking Duck (p.14)

## Mains
Steamed Cod with Salted Black
    Beans (p.59)
Ginger, Chilli and Soy Steamed
    Scallops (p.56)
Braised Belly Pork and Aubergine in
    Chilli Bean Sauce (p.69)

Steamed Fiery Beancurd (p.53)
Chinese Pea Shoots in Sesame and
    Garlic (p.149)
Jasmine Rice (p.142)

## Dessert
Taro and Sago Sweet Soup (p.73)

# For Chinese New Year

Sui Mai Dumplings (p.19)
Fried Prawn Dumplings with Soy
    Vinegar Dipping Sauce (p.42)
Peking Duck (p.14)
Char Sui Pork (p.30)
Hot Chilli Prawns (p.22)
Steamed Seabass in Stir-fried
    Yellow Bean Sauce (p.57)
Egg-fried Rice (p.142)
Steamed Gai Lan with Garlic
    Oyster Sauce (p.144)
Fresh Mango and Vanilla Coconut
    Sticky Rice (p.139)
Chinese Egg Custard Tarts (p.70)

# For 'street food' theme party

Taiwanese-style Nuoromein (p.68)
Pan-fried Prawns and Sweet
    Chilli Jam (p.54)
Sweet and Sour Chicken Sticks (p.12)
Salty Crispy Chicken (p.67)
Steamed Pork and Prawn Siu Mai
    Dumplings (p.19)
Thai Salmon Fishcakes with Chinese
    Black Rice Vinegar Dip (p.111)
Prawn and Mung Bean Noodle
    Tempura (p.110)
Black Bean Mussels in Japanese
    Beer (p.120)
Nutty Chicken Cool Noodle
    Salad (p.29)

## For East meets West

### Starter
Guangdong Duck with Mango
   Salsa (p.84)

### Mains
Chicken and Shiitake Mushroom
   Pies (p.96)
Smoked Paprika Sweet Potato
   Chips (p.143)

### Dessert
Apple, Lychee and Blackberry
   Crumble (p.107)

## For East meets East

### Starter
Thai Salmon Fishcakes with Chinese
   Black Rice Vinegar Dip (p.111)

### Mains
Beef Teriyaki Steak with
   Glutinous Rice (p.130)
Green Salad and Oriental Dressing
(p.147)

### Dessert
Coconut Bananas in Maple Syrup
   and Toasted Sesame Seeds (p.138)

## For a quick meal for one

Zhejiang Mein (p.61)

## For an easy meal after work

Oriental Pork Chops with Chinese
   Pickled Salad and Jasmine Rice
   (p.128)

## For Sunday lunch

### Starter
Chinese Chorizo, Roast Sweet Pepper
   and Cherry Tomato Melt (p.78)

### Main
Peking Duck Fillet and Savoy Cabbage,
   Roast Potatoes and Peking Duck
   Sauce (p.102)

### Dessert
Crêpes Suzette with Warmed Peaches
   and Mangoes (p.105)

# For a vegetarian dinner

## Starter
Mother's Tomato and Egg Clear Soup with Seaweed (p.45)

## Mains
Stir-fried Fresh Beancurd, Pak Choy and Oyster Mushrooms in Black Bean Sauce (p.51)

Soy and Sesame French Beans (p.148)

Egg-fried Rice (p.142)

## Dessert
Crêpes with Red Bean Paste and Vanilla Ice Cream (p.75)

# Naughty fast food

Chinese-style Fish and Chips (p.91)

Lemon Chicken Burger (p.99)

# Salads

Nutty Chicken Cool Noodle Salad (p.29)

Chicken, Beetroot and Mango Salad with Date, Soy and Balsamic Dressing (p.98)

Taiwanese-style Chicken Caesar Salad (p.100)

Eastern-style Tuna Salade Niçoise (p.89)

Prawn and Lemon Wasabi Liang Mein Salad (p.125)

Soba Noodles with Olives, Sun-dried Tomatoes and Rice Vinegar Dressing (p.88)

# Curries for Friday night

Chicken Curry with Spring Onion Flatbread (p.33)

Chicken Katsu Curry (p.126)

Malaysian-style Satay Chicken with Coconut Peanut Sauce (p.127)

Thai Chicken Green Curry (p.131)

Burmese-style Beef Curry with Vermicelli Rice Noodles (p.133)

# Glossary of Ingredients

## Condiments

**Groundnut oil (peanut oil)** This pale oil, extracted from peanuts, has a subtle, nutty flavour. It can be heated to high temperatures without burning, making it suitable for stir- and deep frying. Corn oil can be substituted.

**Mirin** A sweet liquid made by fermenting steamed glutinous rice with Shoju (a distilled Japanese spirit similar to vodka). It is less alcoholic than sake and adds a shine to grilled foods. It can also be used in dressings and is perfect for flavouring stocks and marinades.

**Plum wine** An amber-coloured wine made from fermenting Chinese plums or plum extract. It has about 10% alcohol content and almost a cinnamon fragrance and can be used in cooking or for drinking.

**Rice vinegar** There are clear and dark rice vinegars, made from fermented rice. The clear one is used for pickling and the dark one (sold as black rice vinegar) is used in braised dishes or soups. Cider vinegar can substitute for the clear variety; balsamic vinegar for the dark one.

**Sake** This is Japanese rice wine which is completely clear with quite a high alcohol content. Shaosing (*see below*) or dry sherry can be substituted. As well as a cooking ingredient sake is a drink served cold or warm.

**Shaosing rice wine** Wine made from rice, millet and yeast that is aged for 3–5 years. Dry sherry makes a good substitute. Rice wine is used to take the odour from meat and gives a bitter-sweet finish to dishes. It is served as a warm drink at wedding banquets.

**Toasted sesame oil** Sesame oil is less used in Chinese cooking; far more as a seasoning, sprinkled on dishes before serving. It is made from toasted white sesame seeds and is amber in colour. Although its principal use is not for cooking it can be heated to high temperatures and can be used with other oils for stir frying.

## Sauces

**Chilli bean sauce** A sauce used mainly in Sichuan cooking made from chillies and broad beans fermented with salt to produce a deep brown-red sauce. Some versions include fermented soya beans or garlic. It makes a great stewing sauce but add with care: some varieties are extremely hot.

**Chilli sauce** A cooking or dipping sauce made from fresh chillies, garlic and vinegar.

**Fish sauce (nam pla, nuoc mam)** This one adds a salty pungent tang to dishes. It can be used in cooking, as a seasoning and works well in dressings too. Fish sauce varieties range from clear to golden and come from Thailand (known as nam pla) and Vietnam (called nuoc mam); the Vietnamese version tends to be the stronger flavoured.

**Garlic chilli sauce** Made from fermented chillies and garlic, this is a great stir fry sauce.

**Hoi sin sauce** Made from salted yellow soya beans, vinegar, sugar, sesame oil, star anise and red rice (which gives it colour), hoi sin is great for marinades and as a dipping sauce.

**Oyster sauce** A seasoning sauce. Some are made with oyster extracts, others are just oyster flavoured. It is used liberally on cooked vegetables or as a marinade. Oyster sauce is quite salty, so taste the dish before adding. Vegetarian versions can often be found.

**Shrimp paste** A seasoning usually sold as a block which requires toasting in a dry pan. Some varieties come in chilli oil, ready to use.

**Soy sauce** Made from fermented soya beans. Light soy adds a saltiness to dishes. Dark soy is used for marinating meats and to introduce colour to dishes. Tamari is a Japanese soy sauce which is wheatfree.

**Yellow bean sauce (bean sauce, yellow bean, brown bean sauce)** Sauce made from fermented yellow soya beans, rice wine and dark brown sugar (for colour). It is used in Sichuan and Hunan cuisines and makes a great marinade for meats and barbecues.

**Wasabi powder/paste** *Wasabia japonica* is a Japanese variety of green horseradish, more fiery than the white horseradish. It always accompanies sushi. Combine equal parts of powder and warm water to make a paste, or add warm cream.

## Spices

**Cinnamon** The dried bark of members of the Cinnamomun family, one of the more common being the cassia tree. Ground cinnamon adds a sweet, woody fragrance.

**Coriander seed** The dried seeds of *Coriandrum sativum* are ground to add a distinctive warm citrus aroma to sweet and savoury dishes.

**Cumin** The pale green seeds of *Cuminum cyminum*, a small herb in the parsley family, have a distinctive, slightly bitter yet warm flavour which is stronger when ground.

**Five-spice powder** A blend of star anise, fennel, cloves, Sichuan pepper and cinnamon, popular in Chinese, Vietnamese and Thai dishes. All five flavours – sour, bitter, sweet, pungent and salty – are found in five-spice. It works well with meats, and is an excellent marinade.

**Sichuan pepper** Known in Mandarin as *hua-jiao* – 'flower pepper' – this is the outer pod of a tiny fruit, widely used in Sichuan and in other Asian cuisines. It has a unique aroma and flavour without the pungency of black or red pepper. It can be wok-roasted, used to flavour oil, mixed with salt as a condiment for poultry or pork, and goes well with fish.

## Fresh Ingredients

**Banana leaves** Small sections of the young banana leaves are wrapped around ingredients before steaming. They keep the contents moist while adding a subtle but interesting flavour.

**Beancurd (tofu, dofu)** Made from protein-rich soya bean curd and often substituted for meats, cheeses and other dairy products. In the West it is sold under its Japanese name, tofu. Bland in taste with a cheese-like texture tofu contains B-vitamins, isoflavones and calcium. There are three different versions: silken, soft and firm. The creaminess of silken tofu allows it to be used like cream cheese. Soft tofu has the texture of al dente pasta. Firm tofu is thicker and can be diced and used in stir fries, salads and soups. Fresh tofu keeps in the fridge for a week, frozen for a month, and tetra packs are widely available.

**Coriander** Both leaves and stems are much used in Southeast Asian food: chopped and stirred into stir fries, soups and stews or sprinkled as a tasty garnish.

**Enoki mushroom** Tiny white long-stemmed mushrooms with a mild but delightful flavour and crunchy texture. They require little cooking and can be served in soups and stir fries. Enoki may be eaten raw in fresh salads but are easier to digest when cooked. They are sold in most Asian supermarkets.

**Flying salmon fish roe (red caviar)** The roe of flying salmon, known as *Ikura* in Japanese. It is sold in specialist Japanese stores. The eggs explode in the mouth and make great appetisers or are added to salads.

**Galangal** A rhizome best known in the West from its use in Thai cuisine. It resembles ginger in appearance and taste with an extra citrus aroma. It is available powdered or whole in most Asian stores.

**Lemongrass** The edible stalks of *Cymbopogon citratus* are used widely in South-east Asian cuisine. It has a fragrance that recalls both ginger and lemon and a citrus flavour.

**Oyster mushroom** These white to grey fungi are oyster-shaped, moist, hairless and fragrant. The texture is soft and chewy with a slight oyster taste – great in a seafood stir fry.

**Potato flour (potato starch)** Potatoes are steamed then dried and ground to produce this white gluten-free flour used (not only in Chinese cooking), to coat ingredients before deep frying – this gives an extra crispiness. It is also used in baked goods for Passover (when wheat flour may not be used).

**Shiitake mushroom** Large, dark-brown umbrella-shaped fungi, prized for culinary and medicinal properties. They contain all eight essential amino acids in more significant proportions than soya beans, meat, milk or eggs as well as vitamins A, B, $B_{12}$, C, D, niacin and minerals. Shiitake are a popular source of protein in Japan, and are a dietary staple in China and other parts of Asia.

**Taro** *Colucasia esculenta* is a tropical plant grown primarily for its corms which are high in starch, and are a good source of dietary fibre, vitamin $B_6$ and manganese. Taro is boiled, stewed or sliced and fried as tempura. The flesh may be purple, beige or white but the white variety is most common in the West.

**Thai basil** This herb has dark green leaves with a touch of purple to the upper stems. It gives an intense aniseed flavour. Great in Thai curries, salads, soups and stir fries.

**Thai eggplant (Thai aubergine)** Used mainly in Thai cuisine, the most common are round and white or green – about the size of a golf ball. As they cook, they soften and absorb the flavour of other ingredients. Large purple aubergines make a good substitute.

**Wontons** These wrappers, made from egg, salt, flour and water, are used to make dumplings. They can be bought frozen or fresh from Chinese supermarkets.

## Other Ingredients

**Coconut milk and cream** Coconut milk is the diluted cream pressed out from the thick, white flesh of a mature coconut. Good milk has a clean, white colour and tastes rich, and mildly sweet. Coconut cream is used to flavour curries and desserts.

**Lychee** The fruit of an evergreen tree native to southern China. It has an inedible red, rough rind and sweet, translucent white flesh, rich in vitamin C. Fresh or tinned lychees are sold in Chinese stores and some supermarkets.

**Mock chicken** Made from soya, gluten and other seasoning ingredients and substituted in recipes that use cooked meat. It can be made by freezing firm tofu to give it a meat-like texture, then braising it in soy and five-spice.

**Mock duck** Made primarily from wheat gluten or soya and often preserved in oil and sold in tins. Great in soups and stir fries.

**Red bean paste** Ready-prepared sweet burgundy-red adzuki bean paste can be bought in Asian stores and used straight from the tin. In China it is used as a dessert filling.

# Preserved or Dried Ingredients

**Dried Chinese mushrooms** These have a strong aroma, and a slight salty taste that goes well with most savoury ingredients. Soak them in hot water for 10–15 minutes to soften.

**Dried shrimp** Packs of dried whole baby shrimp are sold in Asian stores. They are deep salmon pink and yield slightly to the touch. Do not buy if they smell of ammonia. Soak in hot water for 10–15 minutes and use in stir fries and stews.

**Fermented salted black beans (Chinese black beans, salted black beans)** Small black soya beans that are preserved in salt. They have a very salty flavour and must be rinsed in cold water before use. Fermented black beans are used to make black bean sauce, a common ingredient sold ready made in most Asian supermarkets.

**Glutinous rice flour (sweet rice flour, sweet rice powder)** A flour made from short-grain rice that becomes moist, firm and sticky when cooked. It has a chewy texture and makes good dumplings, pastries and buns. Ordinary rice flour cannot be substituted.

**Lap cheong** A dried hard pork sausage with a high fat content, usually smoked, sweetened and seasoned. It features in dishes of south China, including Hong Kong, Guangdong, Fujian and Hunan, and elsewhere in the Far East. Spanish chorizo may be substituted.

## Noodles

**Flat udon** A white wheatflour noodle, less than 0.5cm wide and flat. Perfect in soups, salads and stir fries.

**Shi** White shi noodles are made with wheatflour; the yellow version has added colouring. Both are quite fine in shape and are great in soups, salads and stir fries.

**Soba** Japanese noodles made from buckwheat ('soba' means buckwheat) and wheatflour, brownish-grey in colour and medium thick. Soba come in several varieties – cha soba is one made with tea leaves and buckwheat. They make an ideal base for a noodle salad.

**Vermicelli mung bean** Made from mung bean, starch and water. They require soaking in hot water for 20 minutes and become translucent. Ideal in salads, soups or with other ingredients in spring rolls. Mung bean noodles come in different widths, some as fine as hair strands.

**Vermicelli rice** Very similar to vermicelli mung bean noodles. Rice noodles require soaking in hot water and turn opaque white.

There are different varieties and widths, some as fine as hair strands, for use in stir fries, soups and salads.

**Nori seaweed** A dried seaweed sold in thin sheets. It is often roasted over a flame until it turns from black or purple to green before being packaged. Nori is used as a garnish, as a wrap for sushi or other foods, or cooked with tamari (*see* soy sauce) as a condiment. An open pack of nori must be used at once or stored in a sealed container in a dark, cool, dry place. If the sheets do get damp, roast them over a flame to restore their crispness.

**Panko breadcrumbs** Originally from Japan, panko breadcrumbs are larger, flakier and lighter than those in the West. They endow any breaded item with several advantages: they brown better, do not become soft on the inside, and stay crunchy on the outside. Some are also flavoured with honey to give dishes a savoury-sweet edge. Panko breadcrumbs are sold in most Asian stores.

**Sago** A powdery starch made from the pith inside the trunk of the sago palm. Sago can be made into steamed puddings, ground into a powder and used as a thickener, or used as a dense glutinous flour. In Indonesia and Malaysia it is used in noodles, bread and sago pearls (similar to tapioca). Sago can be stored for months in a dry place.

**Woodear mushroom (tree ear, black fungus)** These dried fungi have dark brown to black ear-shaped caps and a crisp, crunchy texture. They are used for colour rather than flavour. Woodear need to be soaked in hot water for 20 minutes and swell to between two and five times their original size. Store them in a tight glass jar.

# Index

# Acknowledgements

This book would not have been possible without the special help of:
Muna Reyal (my editorial director, for her direction), Stephanie Evans (my editor
editor, for her kind patience), Lucy Gowans (designer, for her great style),
Kate Whitaker (photographer, for being amazing), Annie Nicols (stylist, for her meticulous
presentation) and Wei Tang (props stylist, for coming up with the goods!). Most of all, I am
indebted to Kyle for her faith and inspiration: Kyle, you make all of us believe we can achieve
anything! I have enjoyed every moment of it.

Thanks are in order to all the people who have helped me along the way to where I am now, you have left
great imprints in my life – perhaps without even knowing. Here's to: Gareth Williams, Fiona Cho, Stephen
Somerville, all the guys at UKTV for your constant support, Nikki Cooper, Jayne Hibbitt everyone at Great
Food Live, not forgetting Rachel, Olivia and Carl at Pacific who held my hand during my first series, *Ching's
Kitchen*. Above all, thanks to all the great cooks and fans out there who willed my book to become a reality, for
your emails and for your support! I hope you enjoy using this book as much as I have writing it.

Thanks to my staff at Fuge who coped in my absence and apologies to all my customers whom I neglected
during the production of *China Modern* (sorry, they weren't real sick days!). Special mentions to Angela Du,
Meilin, Peter Standing and Ian Booth for keeping my business afloat.

To all my friends and family: you are the greatest. Can't live without Lina and Alex Mahdavi, thanks for your
shoulders and ears. To En-Shen (my brother) and 'Sao Sao' (my sister-in-law), I felt your support all the
way from Shanghai. To my dear parents, for always believing in me and for putting up with my
moaning but above all for giving me my East and West. To Jamie Cho for always looking after me,
I promise I won't do another book (maybe just one or two more)! To my Buddhist master,
Cheng-Yen, and everyone at Tzu-Chi Charity, keep up the good work. To my grandparents,
may the heavens embrace your kind spirits, I am ever grateful for the love, care,
teachings and 'Do-Hua' you used to feed us; thank you for feeding our souls.

Last but not least, thanks to everyone at Hoo-Hing who were
generous in providing all the ingredients; please visit
their website: www.hoohing.com